DISCOVERING U.S. HISTORY

The New World
Prehistory–1542

DISCOVERING U.S. HISTORY

The New World: Prehistory–1542

Colonial America: 1543–1763

Revolutionary America: 1764–1789

Early National America: 1790–1850

The Civil War Era: 1851–1865

The New South and the Old West: 1866–1890

The Gilded Age and Progressivism: 1891–1913

World War I and the Roaring Twenties: 1914–1928

The Great Depression: 1929–1938

World War II: 1939–1945

The Cold War and Postwar America: 1946–1963

Modern America: 1964–Present

DISCOVERING U.S. HISTORY

The New World
Prehistory–1542

Tim McNeese

Consulting Editor: Richard Jensen, Ph.D.

CHELSEA HOUSE PUBLISHERS
An imprint of Infobase Publishing

THE NEW WORLD: Prehistory–1542

Chelsea House
An imprint of Infobase Publishing
132 West 31st Street
New York NY 10001

Library of Congress Cataloging-in-Publication Data
McNeese, Tim.
The New World : prehistory to 1542 / by Tim McNeese.
p. cm. — (Discovering U.S. history)
Includes bibliographical references and index.
ISBN 978-1-60413-348-6 (hardcover : acid-free paper) 1. Indians of North America—Juvenile literature. 2. America—Antiquities—Juvenile literature. 3. America—Discovery and exploration—Juvenile literature. I. Title. II. Series.

E77.4.M35 2008
970.004'97—dc22

2008055169

Chelsea House books are available at special discounts when purchased in bulk quantities for businesses, associations, institutions, or sales promotions. Please call our Special Sales Department in New York at (212) 967-8800 or (800) 322-8755.

You can find Chelsea House on the World Wide Web at http://www.chelseahouse.com

The Discovering U.S. History series was produced for Chelsea House by Bender Richardson White, Uxbridge, UK

Editors: Lionel Bender and Susan Malyan
Designer and Picture Researcher: Ben White
Production: Kim Richardson
Maps and graphics: Stefan Chabluk

Cover design by Alicia Post
Cover printed by Bang Printing, Brainerd, MN
Book printed and bound by Bang Printing, Brainerd, MN
Date printed: May 2010

Printed in the United States of America

Bang BRW 10 9 8 7 6 5 4 3 2 1

This book is printed on acid-free paper.

All links and web addresses were checked and verified to be correct at the time of publication. Because of the dynamic nature of the web, some addresses and links may have changed since publication and may no longer be valid.

Contents

Introduction
A Place Called America

As recently as five centuries ago not a single person in Europe, Africa, or Asia knew of the existence of the two continents that we now call the Americas. Peoples outside the Americas were unaware of the size, the scope, and the lay of the land. They were also unaware of the tens of millions of people who had already made their homes on its plains, along its fertile valleys, up on its hills and mountains, and along the shores of its rivers and lakes.

FIRST PEOPLES

Thousands of years earlier groups of ancient peoples had migrated onto the Western Hemisphere—the lands that today make up North, Central, and South America. But over the millennia, the connections between the lands these early inhabitants of the Americas had come from and the new worlds they made their homes had been lost. The world of the Americas was not only a mystery, it was unknown.

Traversing the borders of Utah and Arizona, Monument Valley is home to the Navajo. Its iconic landscape typifies the dry deserts of the Southwest and contrasts with the prairies, coasts, rivers and lakes, mountains, and forests elsewhere in America.

Many years later a portion of that "lost world" became a country known as the United States of America. Today that nation extends, as the song goes, "from sea to shining sea," and is no longer a secret from the peoples of the rest of the world. It is home to more than 300 million people, some of them immigrants from other countries and continents, sometimes the same places from which those ancient peoples migrated thousands of years ago.

TODAY'S POPULATION

People in the United States today live in a wide variety of places, creating a diverse quilt of urban, suburban, and rural societies. Some live near the oceans that extend along thousands of miles of the country's western, eastern, and southern coasts. Others enjoy living in the mountains, from the Rockies to the Appalachians to the Ozarks. Still others have made their homes in America's remote, arid deserts or even in the cold, sun-clouded reaches of frozen Alaska. The vast prairies and plains are home to others who want a land that is spacious and uninterrupted.

IMPORTANCE OF THE LAND

In part the history of the United States of America is better understood when placed side by side with the nation's geography. In so many places and in countless ways the American topography has always been a key element in the country's history. Not only does a nation's geography determine where people live, it also explains how they live. In its cultural form, geography is about the relationship between the land, its various resources, the people who live on it, and how they utilize those natural resources.

NEW WORLD AND NATIVE AMERICANS

Before European explorers first reached America in 1492 different groups of Native Americans lived throughout the land that would become the United States, Canada, and Mexico. There were several distinct cultural regions. By 1542, Europeans had explored the eastern seaboard and traveled far inland.

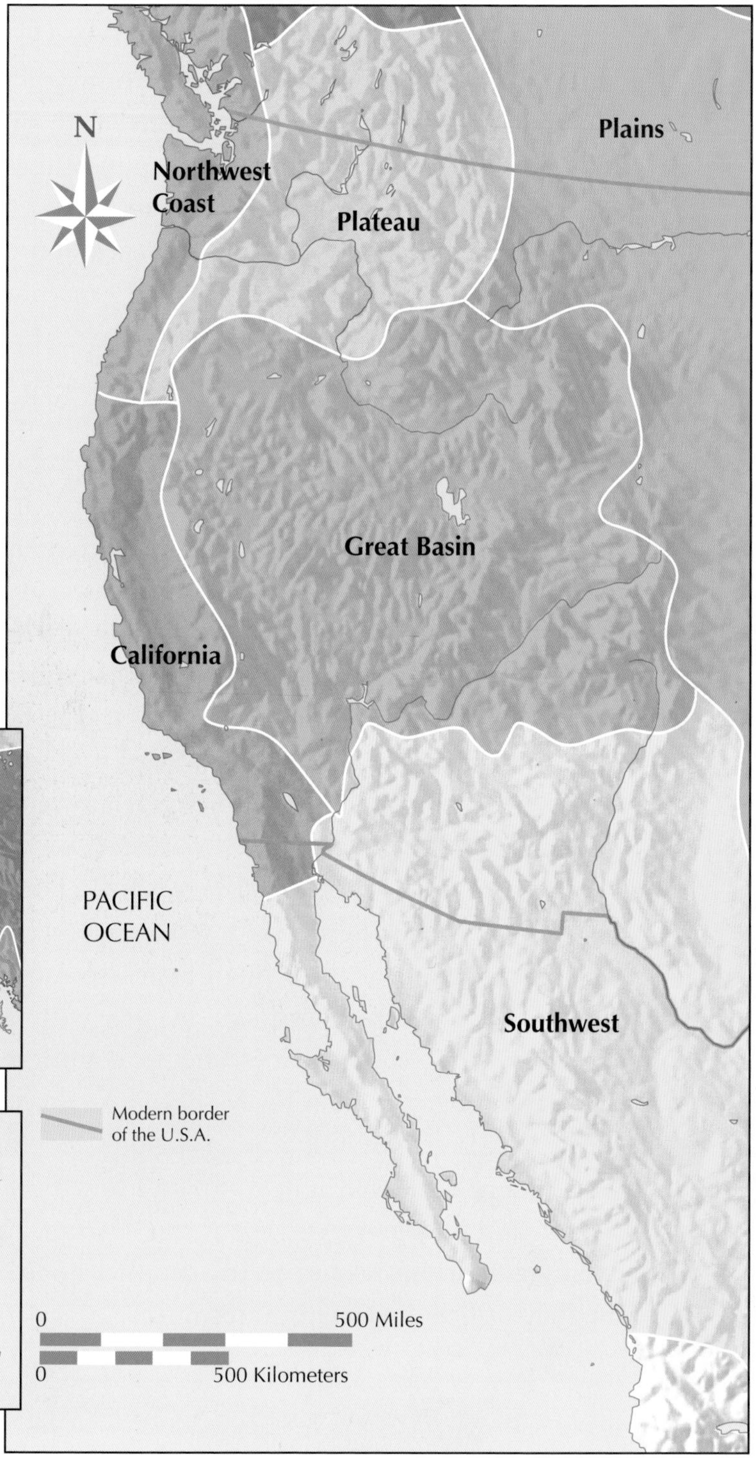

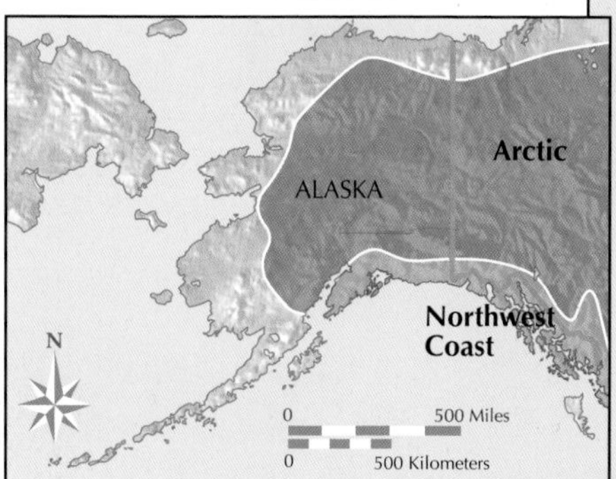

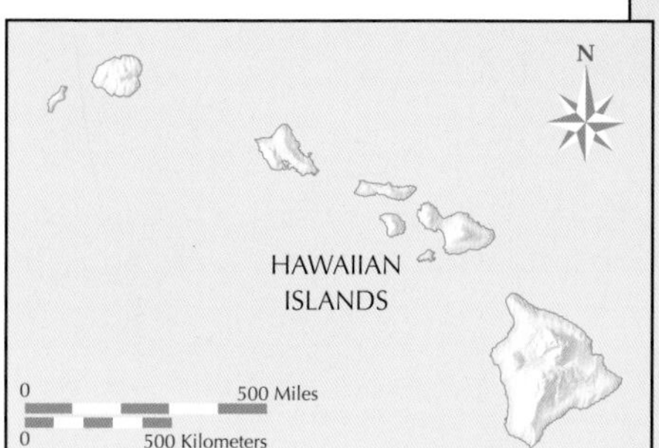

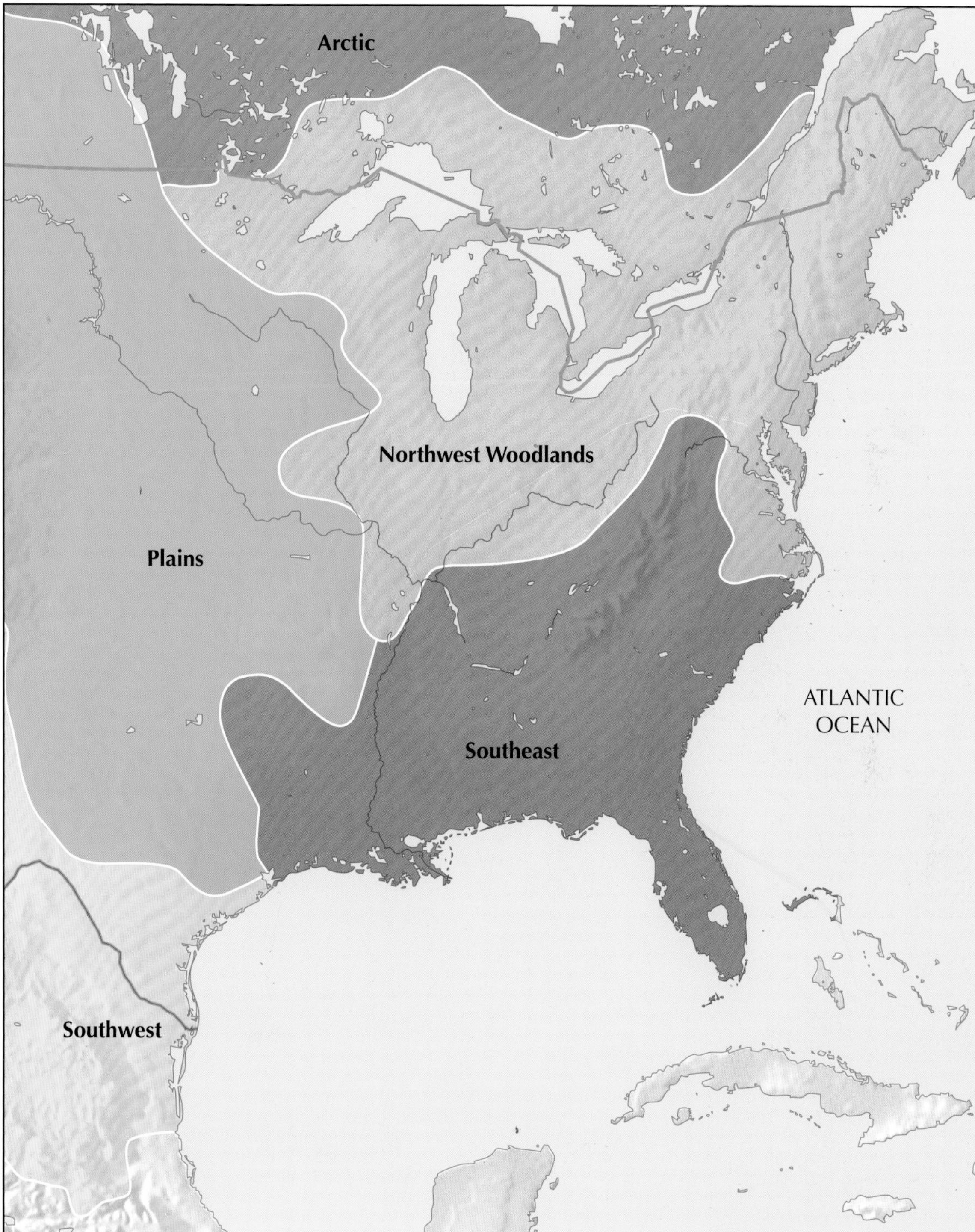
Arctic
Northwest Woodlands
Plains
ATLANTIC
OCEAN
Southeast
Southwest

1

Beyond Beringia

If only we could really know what it was like for the first people who found their way to North America. What amazing sights did they see? How did the land they walked on appear? What plants grew there? What animals roamed nearby? Were these first people chasing those animals? Or were the animals chasing them? Can we ever know for certain?

There are many theories concerning the earliest people to arrive in North America specifically and in the Western Hemisphere in general. Sometimes these theories agree with one another; sometimes they do not. And while different scientists, anthropologists (people who study ancient cultures and peoples), and even historians may disagree on which theory is the most likely, they do agree in general on some of the details.

However else people might have found their way to the Americas, many of the earliest settlers arrived by walking from Siberia (the frozen reaches of modern-day Russia) to the New World via a convenient land bridge, known as Beringia.

A CHANGING LANDSCAPE

The plains, mountains, lakes, and rivers where the first peoples of the Americas lived have not always formed part of the geography and topography of the land. Today geographers recognize seven physical regions that define the United States, but such land formations have not always existed in their present forms.

During prehistoric times the landscape of the Americas, especially North America, was different than it is today. For example, many places that are now hilly were once covered by great sheets of ice called glaciers. The Great Plains that stretch across the central portion of the continental United States today were once underwater, forming part of a giant and ancient seabed. During these ancient eras, no human beings lived in the Western Hemisphere.

The Ice Ages

Prior to the arrival of the first humans in the Americas the region experienced a series of long periods of cold that scientists today call ice ages. During these periods the ice of the polar north extended much further south. This happened because the earth was experiencing "global cooling," which caused more of the world's water supply to become locked in the form of ice, rather than as a liquid or a vapor, such as steam.

With more water frozen as ice, the level of the earth's seas and oceans dropped, and areas of land that had previously been underwater were exposed above water. This natural phenomenon, the cooling of the planet and the increasing of the earth's polar ice, was an important period of change and relates to how anthropologists believe the first people arrived in North America.

Most experts, including anthropologists and archaeologists (scientists who learn from the past by digging up things that early peoples left behind), agree that the earliest human beings to reach the Western Hemisphere migrated there during the most recent ice age. Lower sea levels exposed a land mass between modern-day Siberia and Alaska, which allowed people and animals to migrate from one continent to the other.

Anthropologists refer to this ice age, which may have taken place between 30,000 years ago and approximately 10,000–11,000 years ago, as the Pleistocene Era.

The Bering Land Bridge

During the Pleistocene Era sea levels dropped as huge sheets of thick ice covered much of the northern landscapes. These great glaciers sometimes towered thousands of feet above the land as huge ice mountains or plateaus. Water levels may have dropped by as much as 300 feet (91 meters) compared to today's levels.

The narrowest gap between Asia and North America is the waterway today known as the Bering Strait. During this ice age the low sea level exposed land here, opening a corridor that may have been several miles across from north to south. This exposed landmass is today known as Beringia, or the Bering Land Bridge.

MIGRATING ANIMALS

Along this link between Asia and America the land was not covered with ice sheets, but was ice-free, a green zone covered with thick grasses. Spreading meadows provided lush pasture for the animals that may have roamed from one continent to another. This inviting green belt was likely warmer in summer and drier in winter than much of the landscape in the surrounding regions.

Beringia would have been a paradise for Ice Age mammals. Those animals that fed there as they migrated to the east included Pleistocene horses, camels, reindeer, and bison—a variety larger than today's American buffalo. The horses, on the other hand, were much smaller than today's normal-sized horses. The camels were, perhaps, an early form of the modern-day llamas found in South America. Also in the Pleistocene mix were musk oxen, saber-toothed tigers, and beavers as large as bears. Historian Charles C. Mann has vividly described the Pleistocene animal kingdom:

> *If time travelers from today were to visit North America in the late Pleistocene, they would see in the forests and plains an impossible bestiary of lumbering mastodon, armored rhinos, great dire wolves, saber tooth cats, and ten-foot-long glyptodonts like enormous armadillos. Beavers the size of armchairs; turtles that weighed almost as much as cars; sloths able to reach tree branches twenty feet high; huge flightless, predatory birds like rapacious ostriches—the tally of Pleistocene monsters is long and alluring.*

But even the largest of these animals were dwarfed by the greatest Pleistocene creatures of them all—mastodons and woolly mammoths. Their name describes them—"mammoth." They were huge, larger than a modern-day elephant. Mammoths stood an amazing 10 feet (3 meters) in height and were covered with a heavy coat of thick shaggy fur to protect them from the icy cold. Unlike mammoths, mastodons sported great, oversized curved tusks. These creatures lasted until the end of the Pleistocene Era, around 11,000 years ago. Mammoths became extinct in North America first, followed in short order by the mastodons.

The Bridge Closes

As the lush grasses of Beringia lured all these animals, large and small alike, out of the continent of modern-day Asia, they continued to migrate until they reached the Western Hemisphere. They did so without knowing they had left one continent and moved onto another. Paralleling their movement were the ancient humans who followed the animals, hunting them for food. When the last ice age ended, about 10,000 years ago, the sea levels rose once more, leaving Beringia as it had been before—covered with water.

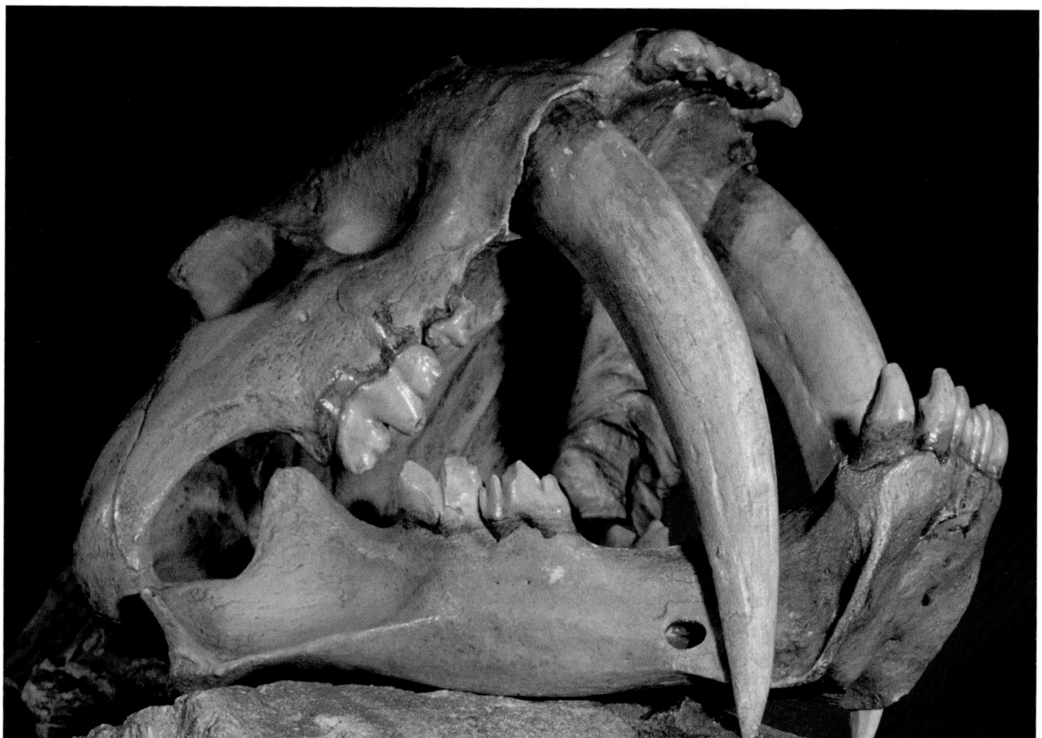

This Pleistocene-era fossilized skull belongs to a saber-toothed tiger, or *Smilodon*. Slightly smaller than a modern-day tiger, this formidable predator used its long canine teeth for ripping into prey.

Here to Stay

With the land bridge no longer accessible, the animals and their descendents could not retreat back to Asia. They had become permanent residents of the Western Hemisphere. They continued to migrate, spreading out across the landscape of their new home. Eventually, the Pleistocenes went extinct. The last of the towering mammoths died out, as did the giant beavers and the small horses. Each passed out of the animal world, leaving only their bones to be unearthed many thousands of years later by curious scientists.

The loss of the land bridge across the Bering Strait also meant that the people—the ancient hunters who had followed their quarry into the Western Hemisphere—could only settle in this New World, becoming the continent's "First Americans."

2

The First Americans

Despite much study over the past century or so, modern scientists still have many unanswered questions concerning the beginnings of human occupation of the Western Hemisphere. The Bering Land Bridge, between present-day Russia and Alaska, offers the most plausible means for getting people to the area from Asia. These migrants would have arrived sometime prior to 10,000 B.C.E. While some anthropologists and paleontologists believe humans may have reached North America at an even earlier date, there is no conclusive evidence to prove those theories. This leaves the safest dating of the earliest humans in the Americas at approximately 15,000 years ago.

PEOPLE OF THE STONE AGE

Life for these early immigrants to America was filled with danger and uncertainty. Life spans were quite short, with an average adult living only into his or her thirties. Given their precarious lifestyle, the population of America probably remained low for thousands of years.

These Stone Age people depended on hunting as their primary food source because they did not yet practice an organized, systematic approach to agriculture. Anthropologists have labeled these primitive peoples "hunter-gatherers." They stalked and killed animals, then ate their meat, and also gathered wild plants, roots, bulbs, and berries. Hunting provided more than just food. Animal skins and furs clothed the hunters and their families. The bones of the animals were worked into weapons and tools. Even animal dung was used as a source of fuel, as people burned dried animal waste.

On the Move

With the importance they placed on the animals they hunted, these early groups of hunter-gatherers were nomadic, meaning they were constantly on the move, following the animals as they migrated from place to place. This is the primary reason why these primitive peoples were not farmers, as planting crops in the ground demands that you remain in the same place to bring in a harvest. As the animal herds moved in search of richer grasslands, small game for food, fresh water, or to escape harsh weather, so did the clans and families of these early peoples in the Americas. This would remain the pattern for prehistoric peoples around the world from the Americas to Africa to Asia.

Anthropologists identify two significant Stone Ages—the Paleolithic Age and the Neolithic Period. The first of the two eras, the Paleolithic Age, lasted much longer than the Neolithic. It stretched back in time to span, perhaps, not just thousands of years, but tens of thousands of years. The term "Paleolithic" comes from two Greek words: *paleo,* meaning "old," and *lithic* meaning "stone." In other words, Paleolithic means "Old Stone Age." In time, the Paleolithic Era gave way to the Neolithic Age, beginning around 10,000 B.C.E.

Spreading Across the Continent

Once the earliest arrivals reached the Americas, they began to scatter about, occupying different places across North America and even further to the south. Anthropologists estimate that it probably took several thousand years for people to migrate to the furthest reaches of the Western Hemisphere. The evidence of human occupation that far south places a date around 7000 B.C.E. Obviously people reached other parts of the Americas much earlier than that.

By 9000 B.C.E. early humans had reached what is now the eastern region of the United States. Some interesting clues to this early occupation of the East have been found at the Meadowcroft site in Pennsylvania, which has been excavated since the 1970s. Archaeologists date human artifacts from this site back to 15,000 B.C.E. and even earlier, according to some experts. South of Meadowcroft, in modern-day Virginia, the Shenandoah Valley's Thunderbird site has yielded human relics dating to 10,000 B.C.E.

THE END OF THE ICE AGE

Once the ice age ended, due to a warming trend, the polar ice caps receded and water again covered the land bridge between Asia and the Americas. Through several thousand years, ending at approximately 8000 B.C.E., the Pleistocene Era came to a halt. Anthropologists believe that this change in environment and climate resulted in the extinction of dozens of the larger animals of the era, including the wooly mammoth and the mastodon. With the vast glacial melt, the land that had previously been covered with great sheets of ice measuring thousands of feet (more than 300 meters) in thickness was left scarred. Left behind were mountains and valleys, as well as freshly cut river beds and numerous lakes. In the warmer environments, plants and vegetation began to spread, providing more food sources.

As the glaciers retreated, North America was transformed. Climates varied from region to region, with each part of the continent witnessing new patterns of temperature, seasons, rainfall, even wind. A sameness of climate had integrated the culture of the continent in earlier millennia, but post-Ice Age America was soon a place of regional differences, tied to differing regional climates.

Through all this great change in animal and plant life, one ancient animal—the bison—did not die out. Early American Indians began to prey heavily on bison and learned to adapt their hunting methods and tools to this fast-moving target. They followed bison herds across the landscape.

EARLY WEAPONS

Since the lure of the early migrants to the Americas had likely been the animals they were hunting, anthropologists are interested in the weapons they used. The most important was a simple hunting item with which they stalked their prey—the stone-tipped spear. The spear was a basic tool, consisting of a length of wood with a stone projectile point attached at one end.

Around 10,000 B.C.E. early craftsmen achieved a breakthrough in stone technology. They began working stones into a highly stylized, extremely functional weapon that scientists have named the Clovis Point. With it, ancient man was able to successfully hunt all kinds of animals, including mammoths, mastodons, and ancient camels. Archaeologists noticed the first of these points during a discovery made at Clovis, New Mexico, in 1932, when they unearthed a spear point stuck between the ribs of a woolly mammoth. The point dates to 11,500 years ago.

A pair of Clovis Point spearheads. Stone Age hunters used such weapons as projectiles to bring down mammoths and other prey, and then as knives to cut through hides and butcher carcasses.

New Hunting Technologies

While the Clovis Point had served ancient hunters well as they tracked their Pleistocene prey, hunting bison required something new. These hunters needed a weapon they could throw quickly, accurately, and at a higher rate of velocity than the Clovis Point allowed. The answer was found in two new weapons, the Folsom Point, unearthed by archaeologists in 1927, and the Plano Point. Savvy bison hunters also developed an apparatus for hurling these new projectiles. It was a spear-throwing device, called an atlatl. Attached to the end of a spear shaft, an atlatl could deliver the projec-

Waves of Immigrants

Scientists do not always agree about when the first humans reached North America. But many anthropologists believe that the people who migrated to the Western Hemisphere from Asia and Siberia came in three separate and distinct waves.

The first wave of migrants entered the Americas across the Beringia land bridge prior to 10,000 to 12,000 B.C.E. These Asians came in significant numbers and migrated throughout North and South America. They spoke a language called Amerind, which was the linguistic origin of nearly all the languages spoken by American Indian peoples into modern times. The Algonquian, Iroquoian, Muskogean, Siouan, Nahuatl (or Aztec), and Mayan languages can all be traced back to Amerind. Even the languages scattered throughout South America today find their roots in this first New World language. This first wave of migrants established themselves throughout southern Canada and as far south as the island chains of the Caribbean Sea.

The second, or middle wave of migrants to the Americas arrived in the western regions of Canada a few thousand years after the arrivals of the earliest wave. These people spoke a different language altogether, known as Na-Dene. The majority of these migrants remained in northern

tile at a greater speed and with better accuracy than earlier spears thrown by hand. These new adaptations helped hunters become more successful in killing ancient bison.

The Folsom Point was in use across North America for one or two thousand years until about 8000 B.C.E. By 7000 B.C.E. the Folsom projectile point was giving way to a technology called Plano. This tool-making era lasted longer than both the Clovis and Folsom periods combined, its earliest forms dating from 8000 B.C.E. and lasting until about 4500 B.C.E. While Plano Points vary dramatically, even from one another, typically they were longer, were not fluted, and

and western Canada, and their language stock provided the source language for various dialects spoken by American Indians in that region today. These dialects are known as the Athapaskan (or Athabascan) languages of the Canadian Northwest. Yet Na-Dene also proved to be the source of other native languages, spoken far to the south. Centered in today's U.S. Southwest (Arizona, Utah, southern Colorado, and New Mexico), the Apache dialects, as well as Navajo, find their roots in Na-Dene. Just how such a language source could center in two regions so clearly different as Arizona and Canada remains a mystery.

The third and final wave of migrants to the New World arrived late, almost too late. They came around 5000 B.C.E. after much of Beringia was already underwater. Until 2000 B.C.E. these latecomers—known today as the Inuit, or, as some Native Americans refer to them, the Eskimos—settled all across western Alaska, including the Aleutian Island chain. They extended their settlements across the frozen north of Canada, settling on both the east and west shores of Hudson Bay. In time these people settled as far east as Greenland. In fact, it would be the Inuit who would make contact with the Norsemen called Vikings, around 1000 C.E. The Vikings—from northern Europe—would represent the next significant phase of migration to America.

some models were notched at their bases. This proved to be the basic design of nearly all later styles of arrowheads used by American Indian people.

Plano technology not only changed the design of projectile points, it was also used to create a wider range of tools. Plano peoples chipped and polished stone wedges, saws, scraper knives, adzes (a hand tool designed to cut away the surface of wood), gravers (a sharp-point engraving tool), and other tools. Innovations such as the atlatl and Plano technology gave hunters greater advantage against their prey, producing more food for the community. This allowed American Indian groups to become larger in size, thus changing their social structure.

THE START OF FARMING

Besides hunting, gathering, and fishing, early Americans eventually found another, perhaps more reliable, means of food production. This was the practice of farming or systematic agriculture. In the New World this shift was centered first in Mexico, but it also occurred in three other places around the globe, starting around 7000 B.C.E. Each of these four farming regions produced a staple crop: wheat in West Asia, rice in Southeast Asia, potatoes in South America, and Indian corn, known as maize, in Mexico.

These earliest examples of cultivation—the practice of growing crops by planting or scattering seeds in or across a potential field—are often referred to as the Agricultural Revolution, a worldwide phenomenon that would forever change how people lived.

Other crops were also soon under cultivation in each of these four agricultural areas. In Mexico, American Indians grew not only maize, but beans, squash, gourds, tomatoes, peppers, and avocados. Central America was also the source for cocoa and vanilla beans. In more modern times, New

World crops such as potatoes and corn were staple foods for hundreds of millions of people.

Settling in One Place

Anthropologists and archaeologists present evidence indicating that the people living in Mexico began producing cultivated crops as early as 9,000 years ago. Maize proved very hardy, producing abundant yields. Not only did such crops produce greater supplies of food for ancient peoples in America, it also allowed them to settle. With the beginning of systematic agriculture, people could now remain in one place indefinitely. This allowed them to be better fed, to build more complex social systems, and to construct more permanent homes.

Archaeologists say that people in Mexico had developed small villages by 1000 B.C.E. By 650 C.E., a completely urban culture took root in central Mexico, where Mexico City stands today.

3 Indians of the Southwest

When Europeans first came to America in the 1500s the Western Hemisphere was already home to millions of people. Across the lands that today comprise the United States, and into southern Canada, American Indians lived in several distinct cultural regions. While not all anthropologists separate out Indian culture regions exactly the same, four broad-based regions are recognized. They are the Southwest Culture Region, the Eastern Culture Region, the Great Plains Culture Region, and the Far West Culture Region.

Centered in the Four Corners area, where the modern-day states of Utah, Colorado, Arizona, and New Mexico come together, the Southwest region was, and still is, home to the Navajo, Pueblo, Zuni, and Apache, among others. The world of the Southwest Indians is the product of the unique environment of the desert lands where they live. Their success is based on how they adapted to their environment.

SOUTHWESTERN DESERT CULTURE

The U.S. Southwest is a desert land that covers today's Arizona and New Mexico, southern Utah, the southwestern corner of Colorado, a sliver of western Texas, southeastern Nevada, and California. The Southwest is a rugged moonscape of painted deserts, snow-covered mountain peaks, and rocky sandstone canyons. Major landforms include the Grand Canyon and the eroded stone monoliths of Arizona's Monument Valley. A dry and arid land, the annual rainfall amounts to less than 5 inches (13 centimeters).

The earliest inhabitants of this region arrived more than 11,000 years ago. These first hunter-gatherers tracked the great Pleistocene animals, including horses, bison, camels, mammoths, and mastodons. By 7000 B.C.E. the peoples of the prehistoric Southwest began to develop what anthropologists identify as the Desert Culture. They hunted or trapped smaller game, including rabbits, deer, lizards, even rodents and insects, gathered wild plants and bulbs, and collected seeds for cultivation. Pinyon nuts, yucca fruit, berries, and mesquite beans were harvested. They lived in caves or under rock cliffs. Some built dome-shaped grass huts called wickiups. For thousands of years, little change occurred among the earliest inhabitants of the region.

Growing Crops and Building Homes

Around 2500 B.C.E. the natives of the Southwest began to cultivate maize, or an early form of corn that grew in pods. They were small and did not greatly add to the available food supply. In time, a new variety of corn, one that was drought-resistant, was introduced to the region from Pre-Columbian Mexico. It thrived well and soon found its way across the continent, becoming a chief source of food among American Indians. Beans and squash were also being developed and harvested. American Indians soon called these three chief crops the "Three Sisters." Cotton was also planted and harvested. These early farmers used sticks to drill holes, then dropped their seeds into the ground. To help these crops grow, they built irrigation ditches and rerouted floodwaters and rain runoff from nearby gulleys, washes, and arroyos.

By 300 B.C.E. the Southwest peoples experienced even greater change. They built their homes to last, since these American Indian groups were now practicing long-range agriculture and intended to live longer in one place. These homes were pit houses, built in a circular shape, and dug into the ground. They featured a roof of log beams, covered over with brush and dirt, and a fire pit burning in the center of the house. By 100 B.C.E. these Southwestern people were busy making early forms of pottery, an art form which is still practiced among American Indian cultures today.

Prior to the development of the modern tribal system of the American Southwest, prehistoric peoples worked hard to tame the region as they developed unique cultures to fit the land and its climate. As the people of the ancient Southwest developed, they produced a series of three dominant cultures. They are known today as the Mogollon, the Hohokam, and the Anasazi. Each made a unique contribution to the culture of the Southwest region.

THE MOGOLLON

With their name taken from the short, twisted range of mountains located on the border between southern Arizona and New Mexico, the Mogollon were the earliest of the three cultures to develop. The sub-region that these early people occupied included the southern half of New Mexico and southeastern Arizona. They were also located in the northern Mexican provinces of Chihuahua and Sonora.

The Mogollon were the first people of the Southwest to adopt systematic agriculture, build permanent houses and villages, and fashion pottery out of regional clays. They produced the crops known as the "Three Sisters," as well as cotton for clothing and ceremonial tobacco. Taking their cues from the prehistoric peoples who preceded them, the Mogollon lived in villages and practiced religious and social rituals in sunken, circular structures called kivas. By 1100 C.E. the Mogollon were building above-ground adobe structures, which Spanish explorers would later call pueblos, a Spanish word for "village." In some Mogollon settlement sites they built as many as 20 or 30 pueblos.

Weaving became an important handicraft, with skilled hands creating elaborate blankets and clothing, which were further adorned with feathers and animal furs. Their early form of pottery was simple. One unique and ultimately commonplace type of early pottery was produced by a group of the Mogollon called the Mimbres. Using local white clays, Mimbres potters painted them with lines of black paint, creating a style known by artists today as "black on white."

In time, generally by 1400 C.E., the Mogollon culture gave way to another, more advanced culture group of Southwest Indians, known as the Anasazi.

THE HOHOKAM

Living in the Southwest during the same general era as the Mogollon were the Hohokam, who developed farther west. The modern-day Pima nation gave the Hohokam their name, which means "the vanished ones." The Hohokam made their homes in the valleys of the San Pedro, Salt, and Gila Rivers of south-central Arizona, where they worked as farmers, lived in sunken houses, and practiced their own form of pottery. They eventually became the ancient Southwest's most extensive farmers, developing complicated irrigation systems.

The most important Hohokam community was located south of today's Phoenix. Known as Snaketown, this site was home to the Hohokam for approximately 1,500 years. Archaeologists have excavated 100 underground pit dwellings there, buildings larger than those built by their eastern neighbors, the Mogollon.

THE ANASAZI

The third dominant cultural group of the Southwest was the Anasazi, whose name means "ancient enemies" in the Navajo language. The Anasazi culture had its roots around 100 B.C.E. and was first established along the Four Corners Plateau.

Culturally, the Anasazi developed through a series of stages. The earliest, known as the Basket Maker Culture, spanned the five centuries leading up to 400 C.E. Archaeologists have excavated intricately woven baskets and sandals fashioned from such fibers as rush, yucca, and straw from this period. As with the other early culture groups, the Anasazi first lived in pit houses, survived as hunter-gatherers, and practiced rudimentary farming.

The next significant Anasazi culture phase was the Modified Basket Maker Culture, which extended from 400 to 700 C.E. This era may have taken place because of a wet climate cycle between 400 and 500 C.E., which made agricultural production easier, resulting in a larger population. By this time, the Anasazi had developed the use of the bow and arrow. They domesticated turkeys, and their fields produced the "Three Sisters" of corn, beans, and squash. The Anasazi were also making jewelry, which included the use of shells, clay figures, and, most importantly, turquoise.

The third stage of Anasazi development is called the Developmental Pueblo Period (ca. 700–1100 C.E.). During this era, the Anasazi built more elaborate pueblo structures that rose several stories above the desert floor. Each contained dozens of rooms that interconnected, forming small apartments in which to live. To provide security from enemies, the Anasazi used wooden pole ladders to scale the pueblo walls and then entered through holes in the roofs.

PUEBLO BONITO

Pueblo Bonito was one of several Anasazi sites situated in New Mexico's remote and mysterious Chaco Canyon. The canyon lies at the center of the 25,000-square-mile (65,000-square-kilometer) San Juan Basin, part of the Colorado Plateau, and flanked by mountains to the north, south, east, and west. Pueblo Bonito is the largest of many Anasazi villages scattered throughout the canyon. Here builders erected walls that stood five stories high and the grounds were dotted with 35 kivas, used for ceremonial and social purposes.

Perhaps as many as a thousand Chaco Anasazi may have lived at Pueblo Bonito. Despite its bleakness and remoteness, Chaco Canyon may have given these ancient dwellers an ideal desert setting in which to live. Even though the region sported little vegetation and had few trees, the Chaco Anasazi were able to develop, according to historian Alvin Josephy, a "center for their civilization—a place where traders exchanged goods and spiritual pilgrimages ended."

The Turquoise Trade

No trade item bartered by the Chaco Anasazi was more important than one stone, which was found in significant amounts in the canyon and beyond—turquoise. This stone became the centerpiece of the Anasazi's desert economy. When worked into smooth, circular beads or into polished rectangular pieces, or even into exquisite jewelry such as bracelets and necklaces, turquoise was considered by traders as far away as Mexico to be, as noted by Josephy, "more valuable … than gold or jade." Traders from California and Mexico who came to Chaco Canyon were willing to pay premium prices for the precious stone. Because of this extensive trade, archaeologists have uncovered such items as copper bells, sea shells, and even the skeletal remains of macaws at Chaco, which would have originated in such remote locales as northern Mexico, the Pacific Coast, and the Gulf of California.

Road building

One of the hallmarks of Anasazi culture was their engineering abilities. Not only did they build elaborate, multi-storied apartment complexes and great underground kivas, they also constructed hundreds of miles of desert roads and village streets, which helped connect them to the outside world and to traders. Typically, the Anasazi built their roads in straight lines, opting to cut their paths across almost any natural barrier that stood in their way. With these linear routes fanning out in every direction, the Anasazi built an involved system of signal towers, so that those living in Chaco Canyon could, as Josephy states, "communicate across the vast stretches of the desert and guide travelers by night." Since Chaco Canyon did not have all the necessary construction materials the Anasazi needed to build their settlements, these roads were used to deliver necessities, such as logs and timber that had been cut many miles away.

The final phase of pueblo building at Chaco Canyon was part of the next Anasazi era, the Great Pueblo Period (ca. 1100–1300 C.E.). During this time period, the Anasazi laborers had become extremely specialized, and included such groups as weavers, farmers, potters, and other craftsmen. Weavers produced cotton fabrics, then dyed them in bright colors, decorating them with feathers. During this period, such important Anasazi sites as those located in Chaco Canyon were abandoned and left to ruin, their desert culture falling apart.

Pueblo Bonito, Chaco Canyon, New Mexico

One of the most elaborate of the pueblos built by the Anasazi is located in the desert of northwestern New Mexico at a site called Pueblo Bonito. It is described by historian Alvin Josephy as "the architectural jewel of the canyon."

Pueblo Bonito comprises a honeycomb of more than 650 rooms, all built into a half circle nestled close to the canyon's northern wall. The city was dominated by a grand plaza, though today a portion of the site has been interrupted by rockfall.

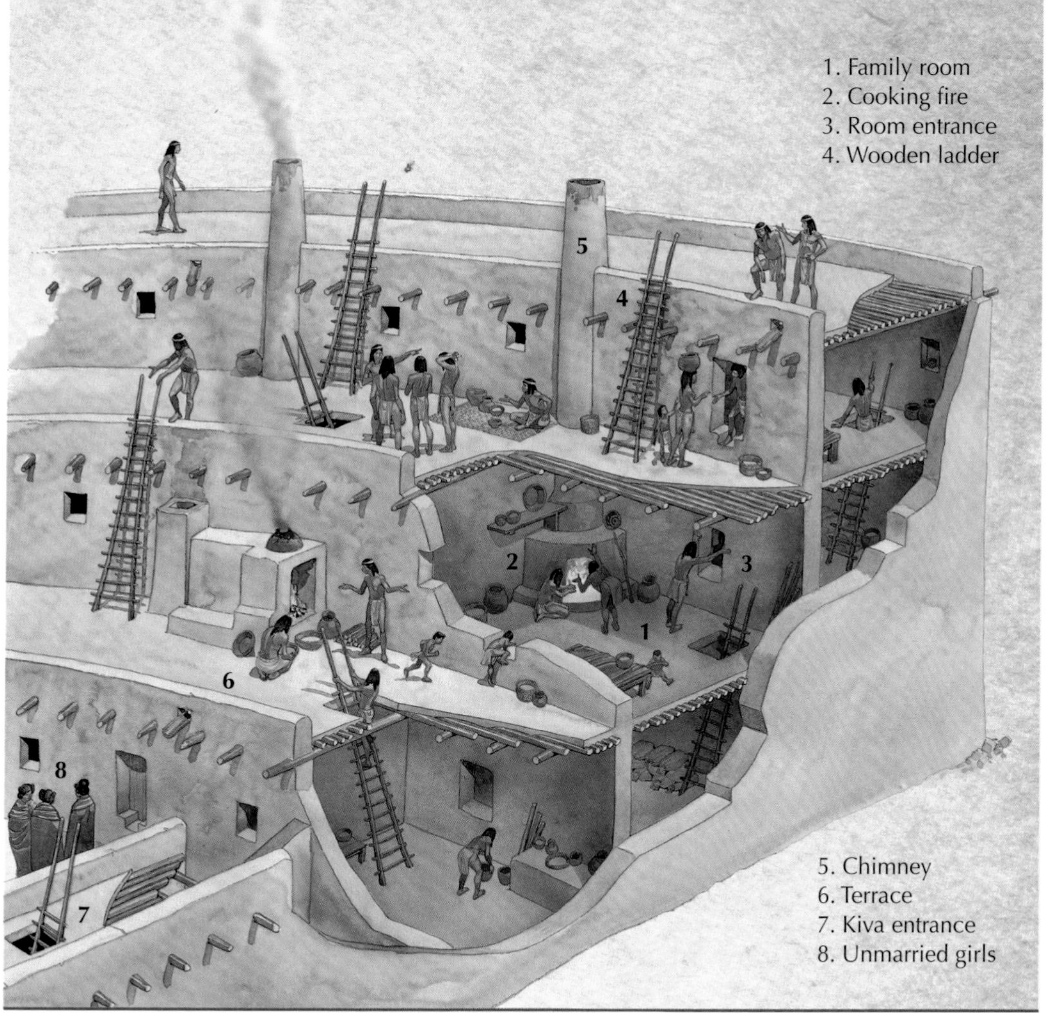

Chaco Canyon is Abandoned

Why, exactly, the involved urban world of Chaco Canyon came to an end is not certain. Archaeologists are aware of other groups of people in the Southwest in both Arizona and Nevada who began to rival the Chacoans in the turquoise trade. Perhaps the regional market for turquoise became glutted, lowering its trade value and forcing the residents of Chaco Canyon to struggle to survive. But another, perhaps even more significant reason for the end of the Chacoan Anasazi, may have simply been a natural phenomenon—drought. Archaeologists note a 50-year-long drought cycle that began around 1130 C.E., which probably dried up local water sources. In Chaco Canyon there was no new construction on any large scale after 1150 C.E. Anasazi clans probably packed up and moved to better living sites, along more stable water sources. Eventually the world of Chaco was forgotten, along with its buildings, which were left to crumble.

Today various American Indian groups claim themselves as the inheritors of the Anasazi, including the Hopi of Arizona, the Pueblo of New Mexico, and the Navajo. As noted by historian Michal Strutin, "Chaco is a vital link in the histories, ceremonies, and ongoing traditions of Chaco's descendants."

The Cliff Dwellers

Not all the Anasazi lived in or around Chaco Canyon. Another significant site was Mesa Verde, where the dwellings were built, not out on exposed desert floor, as at Chaco Canyon, but in the cool shade of cliff sides and rock shelters. The name Mesa Verde means "green table" in Spanish, and the site was located along the Colorado Plateau near the Four Corners. At its high point of occupation, around 1200 C.E., Mesa Verde was home to thousands of residents. (However, despite its significance today as a major tourist attraction in the southwest corner of Colorado, Mesa Verde was not occupied by nearly the number of Anasazi who lived in nearby Montezuma Valley. Perhaps 30,000 Anasazi called that valley their home.)

Today's Southwestern Nations

Anthropologists and historians know only limited information about the early history of the American Indians who lived in the Southwest prior to the arrival of the Spanish in the region in 1540. But, after that date, the record is a written one and the information becomes more abundant.

The Spanish called the Southwest peoples they encountered *Pueblo* after the Spanish word for "village," and that name is still used today. The term is a general one, and includes the nations known as the Hopi and Zuni of the Colorado Plateau region. The Hopis live today in Arizona, while the Zunis make their homes in the western part of New Mexico. Other "Pueblo" groups include those who have historically lived along a stretch, over 100 miles (160 kilometers) in length, of the Rio Grande. These Indian nations include the Tiwa (or Tigua), the Tewa, the Towa (or Jemez), and the Keres. Each of these speaks a different language, but they are all descendants of the Anasazi and Mogollon peoples.

Other modern Southwestern tribes include the River Yumans (the Yuma, Mojave, Cocopa, and Maricopa), located in the southwestern quarter of Arizona; the Pima and Tohono O'Odham (or Papago); the Athapascans, a broad group which includes the Navajo and the Chiracahua, Mimbreno, and Mescalero Apache groups; and the Hualapai, Havasupai, and Yavapai of northern Arizona.

The Havasupai are noted for being the only permanent inhabitants of the Grand Canyon, which they have called their home for 800 years. Their village, named Supai, is distinct for being one of the only two places in the United States whose mail is still delivered by pack mule. The other is Phantom Ranch, also in the Grand Canyon.

The Anasazi's famous Cliff Palace at Mesa Verde, Colorado—the largest cliff dwelling in the United States. It contains 23 kivas—round, walled living spaces. Today Mesa Verde has national park status.

While the canyon overhangs sheltered the villages at Mesa Verde, the lands above the canyon walls were the real centers of economic activity. Here, Anasazi villagers worked the fields, and, according to historian Alvin Josephy, reached "their town by climbing the sheer cliff walls with finger- and toe-holds." Among the largest of the remaining dwellings at Mesa Verde is the one known today as Cliff Palace.

By the end of the thirteenth century the Anasazi of the cliff dwellings began to abandon their homes, the environment proving ultimately too hostile. Scientists studying tree rings have discovered that the years 1276–99 were part of another drought cycle in the region. The threat of hostile neighboring peoples, such as the Athapascans (the ancient relatives of the Navajos and the Apache) also drove away the Anasazi.

End of the Ancient Ones

The final era of the Anasazi, the Regressive Pueblo Period (1300–1550) was transitional, as the Anasazi developed into the modern-day native peoples known as the Pueblo. During this period, tens of thousands of Anasazi abandoned their cliff dwellings and established themselves to the east, along the banks of the Rio Grande Valley. Here, they built new towns, near the security of water—Alcanfor, Taos, Piro, and others they were still occupying when the Spanish arrived in the region in the 1500s. Still others found new lives to the west in Hopi and Zuni towns in modern-day Arizona. As the decades passed the Navajos arrived in the region and took over control of the lands that had formerly been dominated by the ancient ones, the Anasazi. As noted by historian Susan Lamb, "Today, 24 Native American nations regard Mesa Verde as the home of their ancestors."

4 Indians of the East

The Eastern Culture Region was centered in the northeastern portion of the modern-day United States. It included all the lands east of the Mississippi River, extending north and south from Canada to the Gulf of Mexico. The northern part of this region was home to the Algonquian and Iroquoian tribes, while notable tribes of the southern part included the Five Civilized Nations: Cherokee, Chickasaw, Choctaw, Seminole, and Creek.

The earliest people of the Northeast Culture region lived in a temperate climate with distinct seasons. The summers were hot and the winters could be bitterly cold. Yet these early people adapted their culture to fit their environment. The Northeast region stretched from Canada's easternmost provinces to the coast of New England and south to the Chesapeake Bay. Settlement in the region ran to the west where the Great Lakes provided an extensive water system for these natives and their canoes. The land they occupied was heavily forested, with great stands of oak, chestnut, maple, and hickory.

EARLY CULTURES OF THE REGION

Early hunters relied on Clovis spear points to kill their quarry. By 7000 B.C.E. the Northeast experienced a warming trend, resulting in a new culture called the Archaic. During this period, the region's native populations relied on deer, nuts, and wild plants for food, since the great prehistoric animals had died out. By 3000 B.C.E. the Northeast Indians had developed a crude, but systematic form of agriculture, planting seeds, and harvesting marsh elder and sunflowers, grinding the latter into flour to make bread. They also relied more on fishing and gathering shellfish, including catching swordfish off the coast of modern-day Maine. In the western Great Lakes region, they shifted away from stone and began working with copper and other metals, since local ore was abundant. They produced crude tools, blades, spear points, and ornamental items, including jewelry.

Between 1000 B.C.E. and 500 C.E. the Northeast Indian culture developed into the Early Woodland Stage. Notably, several Indian groups began building earthen mounds. One of the most significant mound-building cultures was the Adena culture, named for an archaeological site situated along the Ohio River in today's state of Ohio. Here, the American Indians built villages and intricate burial mounds, such as the Great Serpent Mound of southern Ohio.

THE HOPWELLIANS

In time a new culture developed, called the Middle Woodland Stage. This originated around 100 B.C.E. and ended between 500 and 700 C.E. During this period, Indians developed another mound-building phase, known as the Hopwellian Era. Archaeologists have unearthed one Hopewellian grave mound that contained a cache of 60,000 pearls. During this era, residents of the Northeast planted new crops, such as maize, beans, and tobacco. They also worked with stone, wood, and metal, creating tools and weapons. In their burial sites they included the belongings of the deceased.

Hopewellian people built wigwams as their homes, which were simple, oval-shaped domiciles with curved roofs, covered with bark or animal hides. Inside, the occupants kept several key household items, including elaborately decorated clay pots, which they used for cooking and storing food. Craftsmen carved wood tobacco pipes in the shapes of human heads and animals, and also created musical instruments, including cedar pipes, flutes, drums, and animal rattles.

Between 1000 and the 1400s, just on the eve of Europeans arriving in the New World, those Indians living in the Northeast region developed into their modern nations. Some of the more important nations were the Delaware, Micmac, Illinois, Shawnee, Narragansett, and the Haudenosaunee.

THE HAUDENOSAUNEE

One of the most dominant nations of the Northeast region was the Haudenosaunee, also known as the Iroquois. As their modern-day descendents still do, the Haudenosaunee lived in today's Ontario, Canada, and in upstate New York, where they have lived for over a millennium. This group of Indians was one of the first in the Northeast region to settle in one place and practice farming, which resulted in a move away from almost total reliance on hunting and fishing for food. Haudenosaunee fields delivered annual harvests of maize, beans, squash, and sunflowers.

The name *Haudenosaunee* means "The People of the Long House" and refers to the homes they built—sturdy bark-covered houses that typically featured a barrel vaulting. The

Found in Ohio, this Hopewellian figurine of a man dates to some time between 300 B.C.E. and 500 C.E. The knot over the carved wooden figure's forehead may represent a horn, the symbol of a shaman.

name "long house" was very descriptive, since an average Haudenosaunee house measured 50 to 100 feet (15 to 30 meters) long and approximately 25 feet (7.5 m) wide. The roofs of many long houses reached 20 feet (6 m) in height. Some long houses were larger, at 300 feet (90 m) in length, the same as an American football field! The Haudenosaunee built their long houses so that at least two families could occupy each end of the bark-covered structure, sharing one fire site situated in the middle of the house.

Other Northeastern nations chose to live in a different style of house. The Algonquians of the Great Lakes region constructed smaller, round dwellings, known as wigwams, which provided shelter for fewer people. These were bark-covered domes, which were shorter than long houses, and generally no higher than the height of an adult male. The base of a wigwam often measured 14 to 20 feet (4 to 6 meters) across. While Iroquois men were responsible for building the great long houses, Algonquian women were the builders of the wigwams.

Like the nations found in other culture regions in North America, Haudenosaunee families were based on a matrilineal social structure. Such a system placed women at the center of family life, with children born into their mother's family clan. Haudenosaunee women were also able to hold important positions within their group, including that of clan leaders.

The Iroquois Confederacy

The Haudenosaunee became noted for their unique overall political system. Prior to the 1500s, and perhaps dating back a century or two earlier, the Iroquois established a confederacy of five nations—the Onondaga, Seneca, Oneida, Mohawk, and Cayuga. In 1713 a sixth tribe, the Tuscarora, was added.

The structure of the confederacy allowed for an element of democracy, a league in which each nation had an equal voice. Some historians believe the Iroquois Confederacy may have provided an example for the organizers of the American system of government that was established after the Revolutionary War, a union of states based on the United States of America's first constitution, the Articles of Confederation.

The Iroquois Confederacy—sometimes known as the Great League of Peace and Power—provided the Haudenosaunee with a sense of identity and interdependence. Their longhouses symbolized the Iroquois nations' interconnectedness and cooperative spirit. The Seneca were the symbolic keepers of a longhouse's western door, while the Mohawk were the keepers of its east entrance. The Onondaga maintained the symbolic fire in the center of the longhouse. Inside the house, between the Onondaga and the Seneca to the west, was the symbolic place of the Cayuga, while the Oneida were situated in the east wing of the longhouse, between the Onondaga and the Mohawk. Iroquois longhouses were thus constant reminders of the contribution made by each of the original Five Nations of the Iroquois.

War and Captives

The Iroquois fought as great warriors when Europeans, primarily the French and English, began arriving in the 1500s. Combat between the Iroquois and other neighboring tribes was also extremely violent and bloody. When taking captives, these Indians treated their prisoners one of two ways. They either tortured and killed them, or they tortured and adopted them. The Haudenosaunee believed they gained the power of all those they killed.

Typically, a captured enemy was delivered into an Iroquois village as the villagers screamed and howled loudly. Then the captive was forced to run a gauntlet of two lines of men who struck and cut at him repeatedly. For a day or so, the captured enemy was tortured, which might include being burned with firebrands, his skin ripped and cut.

When a captive was killed, his body would be dismembered by the Iroquois women and cooked. Then the tribe would hold a great feast with their enemy as the main course. (The Algonquian word for Mohawk meant "eater of human flesh.") Modern historians believe the Iroquois practiced this gruesome ritual for hundreds of years before the arrival of Europeans in their lands.

When the Iroquois adopted a captive, the adopting family gained his power. Adoptions sometimes took place to replace a deceased family member, one killed in battle or who might simply have died of disease. Raids launched to deliver captives as tribal replacements were called "mourning wars."

FOODS OF THE NORTHEAST CULTURE REGION

All Northeastern tribes had a diet that was a varied one, supplied through farming, gathering, fishing, and hunting. Farming among the Haudenosaunee was considered women's work, leaving the men to carry out other food gathering tasks such as hunting, fishing, and harvesting shellfish. Farming was difficult, given the brevity of the growing season. Hunting, however, was much easier, since the region generally teemed with wild game, including deer, caribou, moose, elk, and bear. Northeastern hunters also stalked smaller quarry, such as raccoons, muskrats, porcupines, woodchucks, and beavers, as well as game birds, such as ducks, geese, and grouse.

While Indians in the Northeast raised the "Three Sisters," they did so in great variety. They produced 60 different types of bean, eight varieties of squash, and many different kinds of corn, including a popping variety, which they mixed with maple syrup, creating an early form of the snack food "Cracker Jack." Later, Northeast Indians raised potatoes, pumpkins and berries, including cranberries and blackberries.

THE MISSISSIPPI MOUND-BUILDERS

South of the Northeast Culture area, other Indians made their homes in the lands of the Southeast. Many different nations of American Indians lived in this vast region, which stretched from the Atlantic seaboard west to the Mississippi River, a distance of more than 1,000 miles (1,600 kilometers), then north and south from the Gulf of Mexico to the south banks of the Ohio River. Here the rivers, lakes, rolling meadows, and blunt mountains had attracted Indians for thousands of years. While the Native Americans found in the Southeast today speak languages derived from several different linguistic stocks, the majority speak a Muskogean-based tongue. One of the significant exceptions is the Cherokee, who speak a language of Iroquoian base.

As with other Indian regions, archaeologists and anthropologists have gathered limited information about the beginnings of native life in the Southeast region. They do know that pottery was in production by 1000 B.C.E. Around 700 C.E. a significant culture emerged in the region, which archaeologists refer to as the Mississippian Culture, or the Middle Mississippian. The Indians included in this group lived along several rivers of the Southeast, such as the Illinois, Tennessee, the lower Ohio, and the middle Mississippi. How or why the culture developed is not known. But archaeologists consider this culture to represent the third of the mound-building peoples of early America, following the Adena and Hopewell Cultures.

The Mississippian Culture extended from 700 C.E. until the arrival of Europeans in the region. In some ways, the Mississippian was simply another mound-building era, except for the construction of impressive earthen pyramids. These mounds of earth not only served as burial sites, as Adena and Hopewell mounds did, but they were also used as temples, and as the grand platform for the royal house of a powerful leader.

The City of Cahokia

The Indians of the Southeast began practicing systematic agriculture during the Mississippian phase of development, with their crops including maize or corn. Once they began to live a sedentary lifestyle, the Mississippians developed more permanent villages. One such site was the great Southeastern city of Cahokia, located in the region where the Mississippi

A Cherokee Story

For hundreds, perhaps thousands of years, American Indian storytellers told tales that helped explain why things exist in nature as they do. Such stories might explain why bears have short tails, why the inner portion of a cedar tree is red, or how animals were created. The following is a Cherokee story explaining how their ancestors received light into their world, as related by Tom Lowenstein, in *Mother Earth, Father Sky:*

At first there was no light anywhere, and in the darkness everyone kept bumping into each other. "What we need in the world is light!" they all agreed, and so they convened a meeting. The red-headed woodpecker made a suggestion: "People on the other side of the world have light, so perhaps if we go over there, they will give us some."

After much argument, Possum said: "I'll go and get light. I have a bushy tail and can hide the light inside my fur." So he traveled east, screwing up his eyes against the brightness. When he arrived on the other side of the world, he found the sun, grabbed a piece of it and hid it. But the sun was so hot it burned

and Missouri Rivers join one another, near modern-day St. Louis, Missouri. This significant urban settlement site was home to 25,000 to 30,000 people, plus another 25,000 who lived in villages or "suburbs" adjacent to the ancient city. It was a city-state ruled by a American Indian leader called the Great Sun, who demanded full allegiance. He was so honored that common people in the city never turned their backs to him.

Archaeologists have unearthed at least 85 mounds at Cahokia, some as high as a 10-story building. The mounds were built by slave labor, with workers carrying basket loads of earth to the sites to build up the mounds. The largest—today known as Monk's Mound—was erected in 14 stages,

all the fur from his tail, and when he came home, he had lost the light.

Next, Buzzard went on the quest. On reaching the sun, he dived out of the sky and snatched a piece of it in his claws. Setting it on his head, he started for home, but the sun burned off his head feathers, and Buzzard also lost the light. When Buzzard returned home bald, everyone despaired.

Suddenly they heard a small voice from the grass. "You have done the best a man can do, but perhaps a woman can do better." "Who is that speaking?" the animals shouted. "I am your Grandmother spider," replied the voice. "Perhaps I was put in the world to bring you light." Then Spider rolled some clay into a bowl and started towards the sun, leaving a trail of thread behind her. When she was near the sun, she was so little that she wasn't noticed. She reached out gently and took a tiny piece of the sun. Placing it in her bowl, and following the thread she had spun, Spider returned from east to west. And as she traveled, the sun's rays grew and spread before her, across the world.

To this day, spiders' webs are shaped like the sun and its rays. And spiders always spin them in the morning, as if to remind people of their divine ancestor.

from 900 to 1150 C.E. The mound covers 16 acres (6 hectares) and stands 100 feet (30 meters) high. Mississippian Culture reached its height between the eleventh and twelfth centuries C.E. By the early 1600s, the ancient Mississippian centers had been abandoned, the population perhaps killed off by starvation, drought, or destruction by an enemy.

THE END OF MOUND-BUILDING: THE NATCHEZ

Although most of the ancient mound-building cultures had disappeared by the arrival of the Europeans in the 1500s, one Mississippian culture did survive until then—the Natchez. When the Spanish conquistador Hernando De Soto became the first European explorer to reach the region, the Natchez may have numbered as many as 4,000 residents, living in at least nine communities along or near the Mississippi River. Despite interruption by Europeans, this last mound-building culture remained cohesive and intact through the early decades of the seventeenth century.

A powerful leader, known as the Great Sun, ruled the Natchez. He lived in the largest town, Great Village, situated near today's Natchez, Mississippi. Members of the Natchez nation believed that their chief was a descendent of the sun, a heavenly body they believed held all power. This led the Natchez to worship their leader, just as other civilized empires in the New World did, including the Aztecs in modern-day Mexico and the Incas in Peru, in South America. In fact, the Great Sun was so divine to his people that, when he died, his wives, servants, and lodging guards were killed so that they could follow him and serve him in the next life.

The Natchez were a matrilineal society, divided into two classes: the nobility (including the Great Sun), and the commoners, meaning everybody else. French explorers and missionaries of the 1600s called this lower class of people

"Stinkards." Although the two classes were distinctly drawn, it was possible for people from different castes to marry.

Daily Life

The Natchez were a sedentary people who practiced systematic agriculture. Farmers raised field crops, most importantly maize. They also gathered wild rice that grew along river bottoms, as well as edible seeds, nuts, berries, and other plants. With the arrival of the Europeans, the Natchez were introduced to several new foods, including watermelons and peaches. These items ultimately found their way into the regular diet and even, in time, provided some of the names of their 13 lunar months: Deer, Strawberries, Little Corn, Watermelons, Peaches, Mulberries, Great Corn, Turkeys, Bison, Bears, Cold meal, Chestnuts, and Nuts.

While the "palace" of the Natchez leader, the Great Sun, was elaborate, ordinary Natchez houses were simple rectangular structures. The curved roof was fashioned out of bent tree saplings and then covered with grasses. The walls were covered with mud to provide a smoother surface—one that would repel rain—then whitewashed. Such houses were dark, since there were no windows.

For nearly 200 years following the intrusion of the Spaniard De Soto into the Southeast region, the world of the Natchez continued, even if it included regular contact with French traders. In time, conflict developed between the French and their Indian trade partners. In 1729, when the Natchez learned that the French intended to tear down Great Village to provide a place for the French governor's plantation house, they revolted. Although the Natchez killed several hundred Frenchmen, they were ultimately defeated and surviving Natchez were scattered among neighboring tribes. With their destruction, the last of the mound-building cultures ended.

5 People of the Great Plains

Geographically, the Great Plains Culture Region is the largest of all the regions, with lands extending from the provinces of central Canada, including Manitoba, Alberta, and Saskatchewan. From east to west, this vast, empty region of grasslands stretched from the Mississippi River to the foothills of the Rocky Mountains. Dozens of American Indian tribes made this flat, wide-open country their home, including the Lakota (the Sioux), Cheyenne, Comanche, and Pawnee.

EARLY PLAINS LIFE

American Indians have lived on the Great Plains perhaps since 11,000 years ago. Through much of that period, their lives have remained constant. Hunting provided their basic food needs in the early millennia, but during the past several centuries eastern Plains peoples have lived in largely permanent villages, where they farmed, using simple techniques.

The earliest occupants of the Great Plains region were hunter-gatherers, who lived there between 9000 and 5000 B.C.E. These early Neolithic peoples hunted the great woolly mammoths and ancient bison. Between 5000 and 2500 B.C.E. a warming trend nearly caused these early inhabitants to give up life on the inhospitable Plains. During those years the great Pleistocene animals became extinct. With only small animals left to hunt, the Indian groups who remained in the region were typically small.

But a change in the drought cycle caused many people to return to the Great Plains after 2500 B.C.E. Many of them abandoned lives in the Eastern Woodlands to make a place for themselves on the plains. Eventually a new era, the Plains Woodland period, developed, which anthropologists suggest came to a peak between the years 500 B.C.E. and 1000 C.E. Near the center of this time period, between 200 and 400 C.E., those living on the Plains progressed to the point of establishing a stable, semi-permanent village world, including such places as eastern Kansas, Nebraska, Colorado, northeastern Oklahoma, and along the lower and middle legs of the Missouri River from today's Missouri to the Dakotas. The Indian groups in these sub-regions practiced farming, including the cultivation of corn and beans, even as they continued to hunt and gather wild plants. They also began producing pottery, as well as tools and weapons from stone and bone. A small number of items were hammered out of raw copper ore.

New Settlers, New Practices

A new wave of American Indians began arriving on the Great Plains from the Eastern Woodlands around 900 C.E. They brought with them their earlier practices of living in villages back east. These new arrivals typically settled along the more significant and lengthy rivers in the region. They also introduced new crops to the Great Plains, such as squash and sunflowers. These Native Americans did not build tepees, as some of their descendents would, but constructed earthen lodges or huts covered over with mud. Their lodges were square or rectangular, unlike the rounded shape of later tepees. They often built a fence or palisade around their lodges, a practice that had been customary for many tribes of the Eastern Woodlands.

The new settlers hunted bison, driving them over cliffs to their deaths. The practice was for a young Indian to run near the bison, hoping the herd would begin to follow him. The job was a dangerous one, since he was moving in front of the herd. But, as they did not yet have use of the horse—which Europeans would introduce to the New World—it was the only way for American Indians to hunt the tens of millions of bison on the Great Plains. While hunting was considered men's work, the women generally worked as farmers, drilling holes in the ground with digging sticks, then planting seeds and covering them over. In time, they would tend their small fields with hoes fashioned out of a bison scapula, or shoulder blade.

Increasing Contact

A prolonged drought pattern led the Plains residents to abandon many of their villages across the western portion of the vast region and begin making contact with one another, even as their villages remained hundreds of miles apart across the nearly treeless prairie. Through more contact came more trade. Indian cultures began developing larger settlements and a higher level of agricultural production. With a greater emphasis on farming, the villages became much more permanent. Those Indian nations who had previously built earthen lodges began building larger ones, but these were circular in construction instead of rectangular.

Plains Life Before the Horse

In the summer the tribe followed the buffalo herds, carrying their tepees on dog-drawn travois. After the men had hunted and killed the buffalo, the women scraped the skins and tied them to a wooden frame for drying. Buffalo meat was hung over poles to dry. Babies spent most of their time on their mother's back in a carrier.

1. Tepee
2. Tepee entrance
3. Cooking fire
4. Smoke hole
5. Dogs and travois
6. Baby carrier
7. Scraping a skin
8. Meat hanging to dry

By the time Europeans arrived in the Americas, some nations had occupied the Plains for hundreds of years. They had already developed into their various modern tribal groups, including the Iowa, Kansas, Missouri, Omaha Osage, Otoe, and Ponça, who all lived along the Lower Missouri River. Along the river's middle course were the Arikara, Hidatsa, and Mandan. To their south, scattered across today's states of Missouri and Kansas, were the Pawnee and the Wichita.

THE MANDAN

Among those Indians who lived in earthen lodges, one of the most significant groups was the Mandan. They reached the Great Plains around 1100 C.E., having come from the region of the Great Lakes. They made their homes in the territory that would one day become North Dakota, with most of their villages nestled along the banks of the Missouri River. When the first European settlers arrived in the vicinity of the Mandan, the tribe was living in the Big Bend region of the river. The great American explorers Lewis and Clark wintered with the Mandan here in 1804–05.

The Mandan remained in the same villages over a long period of time. They relied on farming for food, along with the usual hunting groups. Their fields produced crops of corn, beans, squash, sunflowers, and, harvested for ceremonial purposes, tobacco. As they remained sedentary, the Mandan began using pottery for storing their food and for cooking. This was a practice and custom of most of the other Great Plains tribes, as they, too, became more sedentary and less nomadic.

Earthen Lodges

The Mandan built their homes in the form of earthen mounds, rather than relying on the tepee design. To construct a typical Mandan dwelling, builders dug a pit measuring between one and four feet (30 centimeters to 1.2 meters) deep, which provided the lodge floor. Above the pit floor, workers constructed a wooden frame that included large lodge poles lashed together. Such heavy labor was usually done by the men. But the remainder of the lodge construction was carried out by women, who covered over the lodge beams with several layers of willow branches, intricately woven together. Then, over this wooden framework, the Mandan women built up a heavy layer of sod and prairie grass, which provided the needed insulation for the earthen lodge. The sod helped make the lodge as comfortable as

Published in 1843, this hand-colored woodcut is based on a painting by Karl Bodmer. It shows Mandan Indians performing the sacred bison dance in front of their medicine, or ceremonial, lodge.

possible, keeping the dwelling cool in the summer and warm in the winter. This was important, especially during winters on the northern Plains when temperatures can fall to 50 degrees below freezing or lower. The average Mandan village might consist of 10 to 100 lodges.

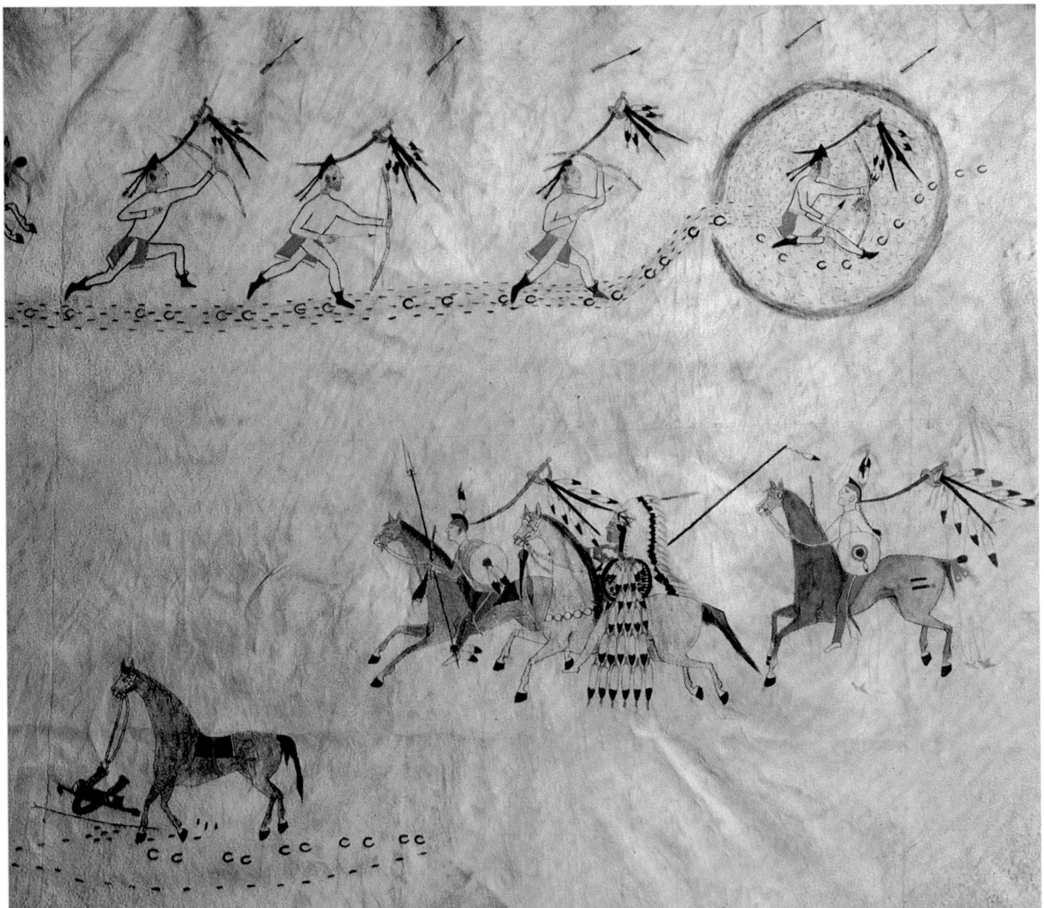

This Sioux painting on buffalo hide depicts a horseback battle between the Sioux and the neighboring Blackfoot. Such battles determined who controlled the scarce resources of the Plains, and also allowed young warriors to prove their worth.

Several families could make their homes in a single earthen lodge, with some providing shelter for as many as 40 or 50 residents, perhaps more. Each Mandan family was expected to provide its own cooking utensils and bedding, with the Mandan "cots" usually spread along the outer wall of the lodge circle. Mandan dogs also lived in these shelters. Each lodge included a central fire site, where a fire burned to provide heat for cooking and additional warmth during the winter. At the center of the roof, the builders included a hole to allow smoke to escape.

These lodges were built to withstand an accumulation of heavy snow on their roofs. They were so well built that many people could stand on the domed roofs simultaneously without fear of the structure collapsing. Typically, the members of the tribe used the roofs as gathering places, where they played games, did their daily chores, or just took a nap in the afternoon sun. The Mandan also stored their possessions on the roofs of their homes.

The Mandan were not the only northern Plains tribe to use the earthen lodge model as their typical home. In all, eight Great Plains tribal groups lived for at least a majority of the year in such dwellings. In addition to the Mandan, these tribes included the Arikara, the Hidatsa, the Pawnee, the Omaha, the Caddo, the Wichita, and the Osage.

PLAINS INDIANS AT WAR

For centuries prior to the arrival of the first Europeans on the Great Plains, raiding and fighting were commonplace between the region's two dozen or so individual nations. Warring took place in other cultural regions as well, but the fighting on the Great Plains was slightly different. A tribe's warriors established a number of military societies and nearly all the adult males would belong to one of them. Young men were initiated into a fighting society when they were in their early teens. The expectations of such warrior groups were rigorous, and followed specific codes of behavior and practice. Ritual in such groups was important and members were expected to learn special songs and dances, and wear specially designed insignia and markings on their bodies, all indicating the specific military society to which they belonged.

Most of the Great Plains military societies were exclusive to the members of one particular tribe, though some were inter-tribal. Warriors were only allowed to join when they were invited by the existing members. An invitation might

Horse and Buffalo Culture

Once Europeans arrived in the New World during the 1500s, the world of the American Indians soon changed dramatically. Some of these changes worked against the Indians, to the advantage of the Europeans, while others proved to be advantageous. One of the best examples of how Europeans changed the culture of the Indians on the Great Plains is the introduction of the horse.

Horses had existed in the Americas during prehistoric times, but these ancient creatures were more the size of large dogs, too small to be used as beasts of burden, and had long ago died out as a species. The Spanish introduced the first full-sized horses to the New World through colonization. As the Spanish established their far-flung outposts in Mexico and the U.S. Southwest, their horses sometimes either escaped or were stolen by Indians. These powerful animals were then introduced into Indian cultures. By the 1680s and 1690s, horses were in the hands of most of the tribal groups of the Southwest.

By the mid-eighteenth century, horses had found their way onto the Great Plains, and most Plains nations were starting to rely on them. The horse changed everything. Indian nations discovered a new mobility, allowing them to travel about more

be extended once a warrior had proven himself in a fight. Many tribes had more than one military society. The Kiowa, for example, had six, including a "junior" society for young men between 10 and 12 years of age. The purpose of such a society was to train a boy for military service. Originally, the Cheyenne on the northern Great Plains had five societies: the Fox, Elk (or Hoof Rattle), Shield, Bowstring, and the fiercest of all, the Dog Soldiers.

Among the Lakota (Sioux), warriors vied for membership in the elite society known as the Strong Hearts. Fighters from this society were known as the sash-wearers. Heralded for

easily in hunting parties and even to move an entire village from one location to another. With this greater mobility provided by the horse, some Plains nations began to rely less on systematic agriculture as their primary source of food.

The result was the development before the end of the 1700s of the horse and buffalo culture. Where earlier groups of hunters had been forced to send runners into a herd and lead them off a cliff, hunters on horseback could lead their horses into a herd and give chase, moving in for the kill.

The horse also allowed hunters to move in greater arcs over longer distances to hunt. All this allowed Indian hunters to kill buffalo in greater numbers and with greater frequency. This caused some Indian groups to become reliant on the bison for food. Ironically, for some, farming became a practice of the past.

Great Plains tribes became, once again, nomadic, moving where the buffalo herds moved in search of food and water. Their temporary shelters were tepees, which could be quickly and easily dismantled and moved from place to place. This work was done by the women of the tribe, who had the responsibility of taking down, moving, and reconstructing the tepees at the next designated village site. They did get some help, however, from the horses, who pulled long poles behind them, with the buffalo hides stacked on top.

their bravery, sash-wearers would advance in the face of an enemy, dismount from their ponies, and stake their sashes to the ground, using a lance. The other end of the sash was tied around their necks. They then fought in this spot, pinned to the ground, refusing to move, until they were either killed or a fellow warrior released them. These warriors were found in other Plains tribes as well, including the Cheyenne.

Counting Coup

Among Great Plains warriors, one of the most unique and courageous acts of war was the strange practice of "counting coup." While fighting between other Indian nations usually included the expectation that warriors would kill one another, many Plains Indians thought it more honorable to shame an enemy than to kill him. One means of accomplishing such humiliation was to merely touch or hit an enemy, and perhaps allow him to live. A warrior often carried a coup stick, which he would use to touch his opponent during a battle. (The term coup is a French word, meaning "blow.") The stick was not, technically, a weapon at all. By hitting his enemy, a warrior could "count coup." The point of the coup stick was to show an enemy that a warrior was brave enough to successfully touch him without being killed. In some cases the warrior carried only the coup stick into a fight, leaving him extremely vulnerable.

A coup might stand alone as a feat of battle, but a victim might then be killed, and then scalped. A warrior usually received an eagle feather for each successful coup. If all three acts—counting coup, killing, and scalping—were accomplished, the warrior received three eagle feathers. Such brave deeds of war were retold by successful warriors around the tribal fires. If a warrior strayed from the truth by exaggerating his deeds, he might face the permanent shame of his fellow tribesmen.

6

Indian Nations of the Far West

The Far West Culture Region lay between the Rocky Mountains in the east and the Pacific Ocean in the west, and included all the lands in between. Dozens of Indian nations lived there, including the Cayuse, Nez Perce, Bannock, and Shoshone in the Great Basin, the Clatsop, Haida, and Chinook along the Pacific Northwest, and a variety of California tribes.

EARLY PEOPLES OF THE GREAT BASIN

West of the Rocky Mountains and east of California's Sierra Nevada range lies an American Indian cultural region called the Great Basin. The environment of the Great Basin has always presented significant challenges to the American Indians who made the region their home, as it is a hot and hostile land. Plant types are few and sparse and animal life in the region is typically poor, forcing the native occupants of the Great Basin to forage for berries, roots, pine nuts, seeds, rodents, snakes, lizards, and grubworms. Despite its arid and inhospitable surroundings, the Great Basin has been occupied by Indians for thousands of years. Archaeologists estimate that human beings have lived in this region since 9500 B.C.E. These early Stone Age residents used Cascade (the earliest style of projectile point), Folsom, and Clovis styles of weapons.

About 9,000 years ago the region was home to the Desert Culture, which relied on small-game hunting, since the earlier and larger Pleistocene animals had all but died out. The Indians of this period lived in caves and beneath rock shelters to protect themselves from the hot climate. Artifacts uncovered from this era include stone and wooden tools, such as digging sticks, wooden clubs, milling stones, and stone scraping tools. The first evidence of basket weaving has been unearthed in Danger Cave in western Utah, dating from around 7000 to 5000 B.C.E.

Around 6,000 years ago, the next wave of immigrants into the Great Basin were early Shoshonean speakers whose descendants still live in the region.

Fishing Villages

Between 2000 B.C.E. and 1 C.E., the inhabitants of the Great Basin had created a sedentary village life, with many of their settlements built near local lakes. They engaged in fishing, using fish-hooks and fishing nets. They also created duck decoys, woven out of local grasses. Hunting was still common, and acorns and pine nuts had become an important part of the local diet, since systematic agriculture had not yet taken root in the region. They remained a gathering people, sending out regular parties of foragers into the greener lower valleys near their villages to collect seeds, berries, and nuts. They used digging sticks to unearth edible roots. When European settlers arrived in the region by the nineteenth century, they referred to the inhabitants as "Digger Indians." The Great Basin tribes also practiced regular roundups of rabbits, antelopes, and even grasshoppers for eating. Food remained a constant problem in the bleak environment of the Great Basin.

Indian groups found in the Great Basin today are the direct descendents of the people who originally migrated into the region, although they are few in numbers. The most significant tribes include the Western Shoshone in Nevada; Utah's Paiute and Gosiute tribes; the Washo and Mono, who make their homes in eastern California and western Nevada; and the Northern or Wind River Shoshone, who live in southwestern Wyoming.

EARLY PEOPLES OF THE PLATEAU

North of the Great Basin lies the region called the Plateau, a sub-region of the Western Range. The Plateau lies between the Rocky Mountains and the Cascade Mountains of Oregon and Washington states and continues northward into Canada. Its territory includes eastern Washington and Oregon, all of Idaho, a slight extent of northern California, and the lion's share of Canadian British Columbia.

Unlike the Great Basin, the Plateau territory is incredibly rich. Its thick forests provide shelter for many varieties of fur-bearing animals, from grizzly to beaver, deer to elk, and antelope to moose. Its rivers are loaded with trout, sturgeon, and salmon, which was a mainstay of the Plateau Indians' diet for thousands of years.

Today more than two dozen nations live on the Plateau. In the south are the Klamath, Modoc, Chinook, Nez Perce, Wishram, Cayuse, and Palouse, while northern tribes include the Flathead, Kalispel, Spokane, Coeur d'Alene, Shuswap, and Ntylakyapamuk. Since these nations lived in the remote reaches of the Plateau, Europeans did not begin making sig-

This Mojave child's doll has been swaddled to a cradle board, a practice that was common for Indian babies to the age of around one. Securely bound to the board, the baby could be strapped to a mother's back, a horse's saddle, or simply propped up.

nificant contact until the eighteenth century. Among those early European contacts were French and British fur trappers and traders.

EARLY CALIFORNIA NATIVES

For thousands of years before Europeans reached the Western Hemisphere, the Pacific Coast of California was home to hundreds of thousands of Indians and scores of independent tribes. Most of them lived between the coast and the Sierra Nevada Mountains, as this region was temperate and hospitable. Overall, however, the California Culture Region features extremes in its landscapes, as well as its regional climates.

Northern California is cool and somewhat wet, given the high rainfall. The southern portion of the region by comparison is warmer, a land boasting deserts with limited plant and animal life, much like the environs of the Great Basin. Still, many American Indians chose California as their home.

By the time Europeans reached the New World, the number of California-based Indians may have been as high as 350,000, including nearly 100 individual tribes. The Tolowa, Mattole, Hoopa, Wiyot, and Yurok lived in the north, borrowing some aspects of their culture from the Indians of the Pacific Northwest. In central California, the Yuki, Karok, Shasta, and Yana lived in small villages, with lifestyles mirroring the Indians of the Plateau. Other central Californian tribes included the Patwin, Miwok, Maidu, Yokut, and Wintun, who lived nearer the ocean. Further south, the tribes included the Cahuilla, Fernandeno, Gabrielino, Juaneno, Luiseno, Nicoleno, Serrano, and Tubatulaba. By the eighteenth century, many of these tribes were referred to as the Mission Indians, since they were incorporated into the Catholic-supported mission system established by the arrival of Spanish missionary priests.

Hunting and Fishing

The earliest Indian occupants of the California region date from as early as 12,000 years ago. They were nomadic big-game hunters, who relied on Clovis and Folsom Points for their weapons. By 7000 B.C.E. the San Dieguito Culture was using tools of chipped stone and stone-tipped spears.

By 5000 B.C.E. California's dominant Indian culture was the Desert Culture. Given the extinction of the large Pleistocene animals, the region's human residents were gatherers, harvesting nature's abundance of seeds and wild plants. They used milling stones to grind plants for food. They also hunted and fished.

Between 2000 B.C.E. and 500 C.E. ancient California experienced the Middle Period Culture, which featured the use of small canoes and boats to hunt dolphins. Indians of this period were building small settlements and villages, making their lives more sedentary. But they were still not engaged in systematic farming, harvesting instead such natural "crops" as acorns, a staple for many Indian groups.

Cultural Awakenings

During the 1,000 years prior to the arrival of Europeans in California (500–1500 C.E.), even more people moved into the region, resulting in a larger number of tribal groups. Depending on what part of modern-day California they made their homes, these tribes borrowed the cultural practices of those native groups who were their regional neighbors, including the peoples of the Pacific Northwest, Great Basin, and Plateau regions.

Pottery was becoming common among California tribes, and clay utensils were used to gather acorns. For the most part the modern tribal systems were fully established by 1300, which means these peoples had already been living in California for 200 years prior to the arrival of Europeans.

Throughout centuries of living in close proximity in California, these tribes did not typically war with one another. They appear to have been peace-loving, not coveting the lands of the tribes next door.

THE NORTHWEST CULTURE GROUP

Of all the American Indian culture regions, the smallest was that found in the Pacific Northwest. The region is made up of a lengthy stretch of land that extends from the California–Oregon border and north to Alaska. From east to west, the region is rarely wider than 100 miles (160 kilometers) inland from the Pacific Coast.

Throughout the centuries, the native groups who moved into this region created elaborate and even wealthy cultures, given the uniqueness of the land, its climate, and its natural resources.

Since the Pacific Northwest typically receives 100 inches (2.5 meters) of annual rainfall, life there was one of abundance. Massive old growth forests, coastal waters filled with marine life, and rivers thick with fish provided plenty of food and materials for building homes.

Out in the waters of the Pacific, Indians harvested another invaluable animal—the whale. These large marine animals not only provided blubber for food, but whale oil as well. Indians hunted these giant creatures in large, hand-hewn whaling canoes, often hacked out of a single giant red cedar. Indian craftsmen might take three years carving such a boat. A typical Indian whaler was large enough to carry a crew of eight or nine men, who used harpoons to kill their prey.

Diverse Tongues

The tribes of the Northwest were never a cohesive group. They spoke different languages and dialects. Over the centuries, dozens of Indian nations came to live in the region, including the Haida and Tlingit, who settled in British Columbia; the Clatskanie, Tututni, Chinook, Clatsop, Coos, Kalapuya, Siuslaw, Takelma, and Tsimshian who occupied coastal Oregon and Washington; and the Cowlitz, Duwamish, Clallam, Skagit, and Lumni, who established their homes further inland in Washington and British Columbia, settling along the many rivers there.

Totem Poles of the Northwest

One means by which Northwest Indians showed off their wealth to their neighbors was to create a unique art form that has come to be known as the totem pole. These poles were typically carved from cedar and served several purposes for their owner, depending on the particular type of pole.

One common totem pole was the memorial pole, which American Indians erected to note the rise in power of a family member to chief status. Another type, the mortuary pole, was often placed near the grave of a tribal leader. A container holding the ashes of the cremated chief was placed at the top of such poles. One of the most unique types of Northwest Indian poles was the potlatch pole. It was created following a special ceremony or banquet as a sign of the host family's prestige or wealth. But the most common totem pole found in the Northwest was the house pole. These highly symbolic poles were placed either outside the front door of a family house or inside. Such a pole announced the special status of a family to all who might pass by or visit. The point of such a pole was to brag or to just show off.

Totem poles featured a variety of animal-spirit creatures, or totems, that were stacked on top of one another. Such poles might depict Eagle, Killer Whale, Wolf, Raven, the mythical beast Thunderbird, or the monstrous bird, Hokhokw, whose long beak was powerful enough to crush a warrior's skull. Including a particular animal in a totem pole was a way for a wealthy person to pay his respects to the spirit of the animal.

This reconstructed longhouse was originally built by Haida Indians on Queen Charlotte Island in British Columbia, Canada. An ornate totem pole, carved with sacred animal-spirits, stands in front of it.

It appears that the earliest native residents came into the region around 6000 B.C.E., during a period identified by anthropologists as the Coastal Land Hunting Period. At this time hunters in the region relied on flaked Clovis projectile points. Surprisingly, a 5,000-year gap in the archaeological record leaves little evidence of a culture in the Northwest. Not until 1000 B.C.E. do anthropologists and archaeologists rediscover Indians living in the region, a culture group they identify as the Early Maritime, which was coastal-based, as well as sea-oriented. They used harpoons to hunt sea mammals, and made their projectile points out of slate.

Farming in the Pacific Northwest

The next cultural phase for Pacific Northwest Indians involved new ways of hunting, both at sea and on land. Even as late as 1 C.E., the Indians of the Northwest were still not practicing systematic agriculture, probably since the region provided plenty of food through hunting, fishing, and gathering wild plants.

Over the next 700 years the Indians of the Northwest developed intricate social systems and became extraordinary craftsmen, who carved everything from simple eating utensils to great canoes measuring 60 feet (18 meters) in length, along with tall fir poles, called totem poles.

7

Europeans on the Move

There can be no significant doubt that the first inhabitants of the Western Hemisphere, including the lands that would one day become the United States, were those ancient peoples who migrated onto the continents of North and South America. For thousands of years these first arrivals created intricate systems of agriculture, hunting, sedentary living, religion, and unique family structures. While it is impossible to know who were the first inhabitants of the Western Hemisphere, it is relatively certain that they migrated from Asia.

But what of those who came from other continents and found their way to America? To date there is no significant evidence identifying anyone reaching the Americas, following the early Asian arrivals, before Europeans made their way to the New World. However, answering the question of when the first migrating or exploring Europeans reached the Western Hemisphere is complicated. Often those who do not know better credit the famed Renaissance sea captain from Italy, Genoan Christopher Columbus, as the European "discoverer" of the New World. But Columbus did not sail to America until the late 1400s and early 1500s. Approximately 500 years earlier, others from Europe had reached American shores.

THE VIKINGS

Today, most historians credit the Norsemen as being the earliest European arrivals to the Western Hemisphere. These Scandinavians are often referred to as "Vikings," the term coming from an early Nordic word, *vik,* which means "bay" or "inlet." But for their contemporaries in tenth-century Europe, the name Viking conjured up such words as "sea raider," "pirate," or "barbarian invader."

These Norsemen were of German blood, and their language was similar to that spoken in England. They were descended from the Nordic people, known today as Norwegians, Swedes, and Danes. They were extraordinary seamen who, by the 800s C.E., were legendary for their navigational skills and their daring, as they plied the turbulent seas in simple shallow draught boats called *drakken*, which was the Norse word for "dragon." The boat's name came from the Norse practice of adorning the prow of their sleek ships with a carved dragon's head, intended to frighten their enemies.

Viking Adventurers

Beginning in the 800s and continuing for several hundred years, these fearless sea-going men of the North raided and pillaged all over Europe. They sailed into every available European sea, then continued up local rivers to reach out-of-the-way towns, castles, and monasteries where they often stripped their victims of all their valuables, including gold, silver, and jewels.

The Vikings even dared to challenge the rough waters of the Atlantic Ocean, sailing out into the unknown, to raid monasteries in Ireland and establish colonies further west in Iceland and Greenland during the 870s.

When Vikings reached Iceland in 874, they discovered that they were not the first arrivals. A colony of Irish monks had already settled there earlier in the century. The monks were quickly eliminated and the Norsemen took Iceland for themselves. Despite its name, Iceland was well wooded with birch trees and abounded in fish and hunting birds. It also featured large quantities of bog iron ore, which the Vikings mined and forged, supplying themselves with iron tools and weapons.

Over the next century, Iceland became a permanent home to a large number of Scandinavian immigrants, mostly fishermen and farmers. The Norsemen also established a local government centered in a council known as the *Althing*, which provided a forum for all free men to speak and to cast their vote. This took place at a time in European history when democracy was all but unheard of.

THE VINLAND SAGAS

All across Europe, the victims of the Vikings' raids told and retold of how their villages had been plundered and destroyed. With more pride, the men of the North told their own stories, which were often tales of daring raids and of how a shipload of Vikings had managed to brave the wild waters of the northern seas to reach far-away lands where they established colonies.

Often these Nordic tales, called sagas, were simply oral traditions, stories told over and over during long evenings around the fire and rarely written down. One group of stories has survived, however, a collection of Viking tales known today as the *Vinland Sagas*. These colorful and exciting stories relate the adventures of some of the heroic Viking seamen and explorers. For centuries, most readers believed these Nordic sagas were simply fictions created to entertain and stir excitement in the minds of their readers.

Today, however, scholars believe these stories might reveal an important chapter in early American history, one that provides insights into the Viking discovery of the New World.

Leif Eriksson Reaches the New World

In 986 C.E. the Norseman Bjarni Herjolfsson was blown west of Greenland by a violent storm and accidentally made landfall on the Canadian shores of the American continent. He did not remain there long, and left without having truly explored. When he told his story to others back in Norway, he inspired another Viking, Leif Eriksson, to return to those still unknown lands, which Eriksson did in 1000 C.E. Historian W. P. Cumming includes the following Viking account of "Lucky Leif's" arrival in the Western Hemisphere in his book, *The Discovery of North America*:

There was now great talk of discovering new countries. Leif, the son of Eirik the Red of Brattahlid, went to see Bjarni Herjolfsson and bought his ship from him, and engaged a crew of thirty-five... They made their ship ready and put out to sea. The first landfall they made was the country that Bjarni had sighted last. They sailed right up to the shore and cast anchor, then lowered a boat and landed. There was no grass to be seen, and the hinterland was covered with great glaciers, and between glaciers and shore the land was like one great slab of rock. It seemed to them a worthless country.

Then Leif said, "Now we have done better than Bjarni where this country is concerned—we at least set foot on it. I shall give this country a name and call it HELLULAND ('Land of Flat Stones')."

The *Vinland Sagas* open with the exploits of Bjarni Herjolfsson, a Viking leader whose ship was caught up in strong northerly winds and fog in the coastal waters off Greenland, perhaps in the year 986. For three days, Herjolfsson and his men had no idea where their ship was being blown. By the time the winds ended and the skies cleared, the Vikings had reached a land of flat coasts and thick forests. Despite the potential for adventure in this unknown land, Herjolfs-

They returned to their ship and put to sea, and sighted a second land. Once again they sailed right up to it and cast anchor, lowered a boat and went ashore. This country was flat and wooded, with white sandy beaches wherever they went; and the land sloped gently down to the sea.

Leif said, "This country shall be named after its natural resources: it shall be called MARKLAND ('Forestland' or 'Borderland')."

They hurried back to their ship as quickly as possible and sailed away to sea in a north-east wind for two days until they sighted land again. They sailed towards it and came to an island which lay to the north of it.

They went ashore and looked about them. The weather was fine. There was dew on the grass and the first thing they did was to get some of it on their hands and put it to their lips, and to them it seemed the sweetest thing they had ever tasted...

They steered a westerly course round the headland. There were extensive shallows there and at low tide their ship was left high and dry, with the sea almost out of sight. But they were so impatient to land that they could not bear to wait for the rising tide to float the ship; they ran ashore to a place where a river flowed out of a lake. As soon as the tide had refloated the ship they took a boat and rowed to it and brought it up the river into the lake, where they anchored it. They carried their hammocks ashore and put up booths (tents). Then they decided to winter there, and built some large houses.

Historians identify Helluland as Canada's Baffin Island and Markland as Canada's Labrador.

son ordered his men to hoist sail after only a few days and set out in search of Greenland. Some time later, Herjolfsson sailed back to Norway where he told his story to the locals, who "thought he had shown great lack of curiosity, since he could tell them nothing about these countries, and he was criticized for this."

Leif Eriksson

While Herjolfsson chose not to remain in this strange land, others were soon caught up in the quest to return. One of those who was familiar with Herjolfsson's story was Leif

The archaeological site at L'Anse aux Meadows, Newfoundland, is widely accepted as proof that Vikings were living in North America 1,000 years ago. Many believe it was the site of the Vinland colony.

Eriksson, the son of one of the first Norse immigrants to settle in Greenland, Erik the Red. Erik had been banished to Iceland "because of some killings." When he wound up in a new set of troubles in Iceland, he and some of his followers decided to flee their new home, sailing to the west, where they discovered Greenland.

Leif Eriksson became so intrigued by Herjolfsson's tale that he and a group of his friends "went in search of the western lands seen by Bjarni" to follow up his adventure with one of their own. "Lucky Leif" became obsessed with making a discovery of his own.

A Colony in a New World

A number of years passed before Leif Eriksson set out to cross the unknown waters to the west. In 1000 C.E. he and a crew of 35 Viking men set sail on their first voyage, bound for North America.

Eriksson made three voyages, the last one taking place in 1013 or 1014. It was during his last trip that he established a colony along the coast of modern-day Newfoundland, Canada. He called his Norse outpost "Vinland." The likely site of Eriksson's colony was uncovered in 1961 by a Norwegian archaeologist and is known as L'Anse aux Meadows.

Meeting the Indians

According to the *Vinland Sagas,* other members of Leif Eriksson's family followed him and found their way to North America.

It was on his last voyage that Leif had an encounter with American Indians, whom he and his colleagues referred to as *Skreellings,* which is translated as "barbarians" or "weaklings." Thorvald Eriksson, brother to Leif, was killed by an Indian arrow. As far as historians know, Thorvald was the first European killed in the New World by American Indians.

Once a colony was established in eastern maritime Canada, Norse settlers, including men, women, and children, arrived to farm. The explorer Thorfin Karlsefni and his wife Gudrid (whose first husband had been yet another brother to Leif Eriksson), made their home in Vinland. Their child Snorri was the first European to be born in North America.

As for the Viking colonizing in the New World, the Norse people remained in North America for a few hundred years, but eventually abandoned their American settlements in the thirteenth century, driven largely by a colder turn in the general weather pattern, which made traveling across the North Atlantic difficult, especially for families. But this early contact by Europeans in the lands that would one day be known as North America predated the discoveries made by Christopher Columbus by five centuries!

THE TRAVELS OF MARCO POLO

The Vikings sailed under primitive conditions in search of lands to colonize, but most Europeans of the eleventh, twelfth, and thirteenth centuries preferred to remain close to their homes. They were not interested in attempting overland treks to remote locales or long voyages into uncharted waters where, according to popular legends of the European Middle Ages, sea monsters lay in waiting for some hapless ship. Instead, Europeans contented themselves with other activities they thought equally important, such as building towering cathedrals and medieval stone castles.

However, some Europeans during the High Middle Ages (1000–1300) made significant treks and voyages. Christian military expeditions set out from western Europe to win the Holy Land from the Muslims. One individual long-distance traveler was Marco Polo. Few men of his time are better known today for their exploratory journeys, some of which landed him in China and other faraway kingdoms of Asia.

Marco Polo's Early Years

Marco Polo was born in Venice in 1254, the son of Nicolo Polo, a successful merchant, who raised his son with the expectation that he, too, would be a merchant. When Marco was only a boy, his father, along with an uncle named Maffeo, went on an extended trading mission to China, where they met the great Kublai Khan, the emperor.

When Marco was 17 he joined his father and uncle on their next trip to China. The men set sail across the eastern Mediterranean to Palestine, then rode camels to the Persian port of Hormuz. Over the next three years, the Polos continued eastward, traveling through territory that included modern-day Iran, Afghanistan, Turkestan, and other Middle and Far Eastern states, until they reached the Chinese city of Shang-tu, the home of Kublai Khan's great palace.

Kublai Khan

Marco became a favorite of the Khan, who sent him off on secondary trade expeditions throughout his empire. His Chinese travels included trips to southern and eastern provinces, and possibly into parts of Southeast Asia and India. For three years, Marco served as a high government official in the Chinese city of Yangzhou. During his travels, Marco Polo kept a personal journal of the places he visited, the people he met, and the things he saw. He was able to accumulate a vast amount of information, since he and his kinsmen remained in China for the next 20 years.

The three Polos did not finally leave the Khan's kingdom until 1292, when Marco was nearly 40 years of age. The Great Khan had requested the departing Venetians to escort a young princess on her journey to his great-nephew Arghun, the Mongol ruler of Persia, whom she was to wed. The Polos and their accompanying party sailed to Singapore, then north to Sumatra and around the southern tip of India. From there it was on to the Arabian Sea to Hormuz to Constantinople, then Venice. They reached their homes in Venice in 1295, having traveled 15,000 miles (24,000 kilometers) in 24 years. When they arrived, they could not yet have known that the Great Khan had died following their departure.

Their years in the court of the Great Khan paid handsomely. They returned with large caches of valuable trade goods from the East, including ivories, jewels, porcelain, silks, jade, and spices, the latter being highly prized at that time in Europe. But their homecoming was marred by a war between Venice and Genoa, a longtime trade rival. Marco joined the conflict and was later captured and jailed.

Birth of an Autobiography

During his time in prison, Marco Polo met a fellow prisoner, a popular writer named Rustichello of Pisa. According to the story, the middle-aged Marco told his story to Rustichello, who translated it into Old French, the standard written language of Italy during the thirteenth century. The result was the publication of Marco Polo's personal narrative, *Description of the World,* completed in 1298. Later versions went by the titles *The Book of Marvels* and *The Travels of Marco Polo.*

What Marco Polo told in his book amounted to a prolonged adventure in lands far, far away. He described the Khan's postal system, which included a vast system of courier stations, with riders on horseback relaying messages from one station to another—a form of Chinese Pony Express. He told about the Chinese practice of using "black stones" for fuel, a reference to coal, which was not in use in Europe. Marco related how the Chinese used paper money, made of mulberry bark. He also described the various social customs he witnessed during his years of travel. The book stimulated European interest in Asia and helped bring to Europe such Chinese inventions as papermaking and printing.

This illumination from a fifteenth-century manuscript of *The Travels of Marco Polo* shows Marco Polo, his father, and his uncle setting sail from Venice in 1271 for the court of the Chinese emperor, Kublai Khan.

Polo was freed following the establishment of peace between Venice and Genoa in 1299 but died five years later. He continued to have a distinct influence on the future of Europe and of the Western Hemisphere.

IGNITING A SPARK

Although Polo's manuscript was written during the late 1290s, there was no means of mass printing at the time, so the ultimate impact of his text was not immediate. In fact, the first printed edition of Marco Polo's book of his travels did not appear until 1477. At that time, eager merchants, traders, ship captains, would-be explorers, and mapmakers read the book enthusiastically, some gaining inspiration from Marco's adventures. One of them was Genoan Christopher Columbus.

Spreading the Word

The fifteenth century was an exciting time in European history. A German printer named Johannes Gutenberg invented a printing press that used movable type, making books available to more people. Other changes and radical departures from the past were also shaping up. It was the time of the Renaissance, a new social, educational, philosophical, and artistic movement that originated in the Italian city states, such as Venice, Rome, and Florence. This great wave of change was brought about, in part, by a new level of wealth that was spreading across Europe. Merchants, especially Italian traders and buyers, were expanding into foreign markets, just as the pioneering Polos had done two centuries earlier. They were trying to gain access to the exotic trade goods of Africa, the Middle East, and even faraway China.

Many of the newly rich merchant class not only plowed their profits back into additional business efforts, they also became patrons, sponsoring a new emphasis on learning.

New schools and educational centers were established. Scholars went in search of knowledge that had been collected in the past, some of which had been lost over time. They studied the writings of earlier Greek, Roman, Persian, Syrian, and Egyptian writers, philosophers, scientists, and essayists.

Scientific Advances

This renewal of interest in knowledge and learning led to a newly educated class in Europe, who began looking at the world differently than their contemporaries. They were introduced to the work of a Hellenistic writer, Eratosthenes, who had lived more than two centuries before Christ. He accurately estimated the size of the earth. He and others declared the earth to be round, not flat, as some believed.

By 1492 a German geographer and mapmaker, Martin Behaim, had built one of the first true round globes in the history of the world. While his placement of the continents was less than exact (he could not even have known of the Western Hemisphere), it was the start of a new way of looking at the world. In addition ancient maps were unearthed and new maps drawn.

As a result of all this rediscovered knowledge, plus the development of new ways of examining and interpreting the natural world, Europeans began to think differently, spurring a new generation of merchants, discoverers, explorers, and sailing men.

8

Columbus and the New World

By the 1400s Europeans were expanding their horizons to greater and greater distances. Traders and merchants vied for the great profits that lay in trade with the Orient. Exotic goods from faraway lands could be bought directly from Eastern traders, providing Europeans with greater access to gold, silver, ivory, and silks. But while each of these expensive commodities was eagerly sought after, there may have been an even more important trade good that Europeans hungered after—food.

All over Europe, people ate food that was less than appealing. There was no means of refrigeration, so while Europeans generally had food available, they had few ways to keep it fresh or to make it taste good. They simply did not have in abundance the spices so readily available in the Far East that could flavor and season foods. Things were so bad in Europe that many people had become accustomed to having food reach their tables in a tasteless and semi-rancid state.

Europeans had known for centuries of the exotic, taste-altering spices found in Persia, China, India, and a small island chain in the South Pacific called the Moluccas, commonly referred to as the Spice Islands. During the Late Middle Ages (1300–1500), western Europeans paid a premium for Asian spices sold to them by Venetian merchants who gained access through middlemen: traders from Alexandria, Egypt, or in Constantinople, the capital of the Byzantine Empire. Europeans could not get the spices directly, because sailing directly to Asia was costly and dangerous during the late 1400s. Besides, there was no direct all-water route from western Europe to the East. Sailing from Europe to Asia would require following a course around the continent of Africa. No one in Renaissance Europe had ever sailed far enough south to reach the southern tip of Africa and continue round it to reach the Orient. But some enterprising individuals were working to make such a discovery.

HENRY THE NAVIGATOR

Prince Henry the Navigator was born the third son of King John I of Portugal in 1394. Although he was not an actual seafarer or explorer, he created a school where explorers and sea captains could be trained using the latest maps of the world. Henry's school was a gathering place for cartographers, men who create and study maps. The prince encouraged teachers, scholars, mapmakers, geographers, sea captains, merchants, and mathematicians to come to his court and pool their resources, knowledge, and other information. Through their combined efforts, Henry's school discovered the Madeiras, the Azores, and the Cape Verde Islands. These island groups and their important ports in the Atlantic provided ship crews with fresh water and food.

But the most important goal of Henry's school was the exploration of the West African coast. Explorations of this region did not begin at Henry's school, but had been going on since the early 1300s. By his time trading colonies had been established in West Africa, but no one had reached the southern tip of the continent. As late as 1460, the year that Henry died, sea captains had only sailed as far south as modern-day Sierra Leone.

BARTOLOMEU DIAS

Although Henry did not live to see his explorers reach the southern tip of Africa, the next generation of Portuguese explorers would see success. One important fellow was Bartolomeu Dias.

Born just three years before Henry's death, Dias was chosen by King John II to mount an expedition to discover the southern end of the African continent. In 1486 he and his men sailed down the west coast of Africa until they reached the mouth of the Congo River, which Portuguese seamen had only reached the previous year. Continuing on, he reached the mouth of the Orange River, located in today's South Africa. But a storm blew him away from landfall and continued to batter his boats for nearly two weeks.

Rounding the Cape

Once calmer weather set in, Dias sailed east to reach land. When he found no land, he sailed north, landing at Bahia dos Vaqueiros, known as modern-day Mosselbaai (Mossel Bay). By reaching this point of land, Dias had at last reached the southern tip of Africa. But he did not stop there. Intent on continuing his explorations into new waters, he sailed farther east, reaching Aloga Bay, where Port Elizabeth stands today. A little further on, he reached Great Fish River, which he named for one of his ships, Rio Infante. Here, his explorations ended. His crewmen, tired and fearful that they might not get home, threatened Dias with a sit-down strike, causing him to abandon any plans to continue further east. The ships sailed back to Lisbon. The entire round trip voyage had taken 16 months.

In detail, Dias described to King John what he had seen and where he had gone. He told the king about the southern tip of Africa, especially the cape of land he had reached during his return trip (the great storm had pushed him past it the first time, sight unseen). It was then that King John chose to name it the Cape of Good Hope.

Dias's discovery appeared a good sign to the Portuguese court that even greater discoveries might soon be made, putting Asia and its spices within reach. As for Dias, he did not return to exploring the coast of Africa until 1497. But on that voyage, he sailed in the company of another explorer, Vasco da Gama, as his subordinate officer. In 1500, while on yet another voyage to Africa, Dias died when his ship went down in a violent sea storm.

DA GAMA REACHES THE EAST

Vasco da Gama was the sea captain who finally realized the dream of Prince Henry the Navigator. He was born at Sines, Portugal, perhaps in the year 1469, the son of a sea captain who had ties to the king.

In mid-summer 1497 Vasco da Gama, along with his brother Paulo and a crew of 150, set sail in four ships. They sailed to the south, bound for the African coast. The voyage progressed well and the ships reached Mossel Bay, east of the Cape of Good Hope, on Christmas Day. By the following March, they were on the eastern side of Africa, making contact with Arab traders in Mozambique.

Within two months, da Gama's ships reached Calicut (Kozhikode), India. After so many decades of slow progress along the coast of Africa, a Portuguese sea captain had finally completed the journey from western Europe to Asia.

The Significance for Trade

The port of Calicut was stuffed with spices—the ultimate goal of the search for an all-water route to the East. Calicut had served as an important port since the 1300s. Previously, trade out of the port had been controlled by Arabs, but da Gama was able to make an agreement with the local Indian rulers to coordinate a direct sea-going trade connection with the Portuguese. For the first time, European traders could completely bypass the land trade routes and the middlemen who drove up the prices of eastern goods, including spices.

Da Gama loaded his ships with spices and returned home, reaching Lisbon in July 1499. Three years later da Gama sailed again for India, this time with a fleet of 25 ships. When he returned to Portugal after reaching India, his ships were laden with spices. Most of the cargo was pepper—more than 2,100 tons (1,900 metric tons) of the stuff. Da Gama introduced so much pepper into Lisbon that the price of that single spice dropped by 90 percent! Almost immediately, the new trade connection between Portugal and India was paying off dramatically. This was da Gama's final voyage, however. Having made his name as an explorer and trader, he served as an advisor to two kings for the next 20 years until he died, as the Viceroy of India, in 1525, in the land he had reached so many years earlier.

SPAIN AND COLUMBUS

During the second half of the fifteenth century, Portugal was not the only kingdom on the Iberian Peninsula intent on discovering an all-water route to the Spice Islands of Asia. Its neighbor, Spain, was also sending sea captains and traders into the same waters. In 1492 King Ferdinand and Queen Isabella of Spain decided to sponsor a young sailor and cartographer from Genoa, named Christopher Columbus, who was intent on sailing to the Spice Islands and to

A portrait of Christopher Columbus painted about 50 years after his voyages to the New World. Devoutly pious, his motive for exploration was to spread the Catholic faith. His sponsors shared this objective.

China. Columbus had promised the king and queen that he could easily reach the Orient—but by sailing west, not east.

On August 3, 1492 Columbus and his crew of 100 men set sail, taking a wind to the west. They sailed on three ships: the largest of the three, named the *Santa Maria,* and two smaller vessels, the *Pinta* and the *Santa Clara.* The *Santa*

Christopher Columbus

Christopher Columbus was the oldest of five siblings, including two brothers, Bartholomew and Diego, who sailed with him on his later voyages. He grew up on the sea, living in the port of Genoa in Italy.

By age 19 Columbus left home, joining the crew of a Genoese galley. His journeys took him as far from home as Iceland, where he saw a pair of bodies wash up on shore. They were probably Inuits, or Eskimos, but Columbus thought they looked Chinese. Years later, he remembered what he had seen and it probably served as a "proof" to him that China lay to the west of Europe.

By the mid-1470s Columbus had decided that the distance between Europe and Asia was less then anyone thought. He devised a plan to sail directly west from the Iberian Peninsula, certain that Marco Polo's China lay only 5,000 nautical miles (9,300 kilometers) due west. This meant that sailing around thousands of miles of African coast was unnecessary and a waste of time. (In reality, the distance from the Canary Islands, which lie west of Lisbon, to China is closer to 11,000 nautical miles, or 20,400 km.)

Columbus longed to prove that his theory was right. In the early 1480s he began searching for a sponsor,

Clara measured only 55 feet (17 meters) in length, so it was nicknamed the *Nina,* Spanish for "little one."

Nine days out, the fleet reached the Canary Islands off the west coast of northwest Africa. From there, the unknown lay ahead. A fair trade wind seemed to always blow west,

(continued on page 96)

but was turned down by all. Columbus tried to get an audience with King Ferdinand and Queen Isabella of Spain in 1485, but he had to wait an entire year before Isabella agreed to give him a hearing. While Isabella liked Columbus, she only recommended forming a commission to study his ideas. Four years later the commission determined that Columbus had missed the mark on his distances by thousands of miles. However, the queen suggested that he should come back a year later and make another request for sponsorship.

In December 1491, an undaunted Columbus did as the queen had suggested. This time another commission decided to give the Genoan an opportunity to prove himself right. But when Columbus demanded that he should be granted 10 percent of all the trade profits resulting from his voyage to the Orient, Ferdinand and Isabella balked. Having failed again, a disheartened Columbus decided to pack up his maps, charts, and personal belongings, and leave Spain.

On the day that the monarchs informed Columbus they would not sponsor him, Luis de Santangel, the keeper of the king's privy purse, met with Isabella and convinced her that Columbus might represent a significant opportunity for her kingdom and to spread the Gospel. As the queen's mind changed, so did history.

Naming the New World "America"

While historians give the credit for the European "discovery" of the Western Hemisphere to Christopher Columbus, his name would not be used to identify those lands. Instead, the Americas are named after another Italian explorer, a seaman of insignificance to history overall, but whose name has been used on world maps for hundreds of years—Amerigo Vespucci.

Vespucci was an Italian merchant, born in 1454 in Florence. He came from an important family and was educated by an uncle who was a Dominican priest. Even as a boy, Amerigo was interested in astronomy and was widely read, and he studied for a time under the great Renaissance painter and sculptor, Michelangelo. As a young man, Vespucci traveled to other countries, including Spain, on behalf of various bankers.

While living in Seville and Cadiz, Vespucci worked for a firm that provided financial backing for lengthy sea voyages. He gained knowledge of ships and studied navigation. He would later claim that he sailed on a ship to the New World just five years after Columbus' first voyage, but the historical record is scant and historians are not certain that he actually made that early trip. However, his voyage to America two years later (in 1499) is documented and unquestioned by historians.

During one such voyage to the New World, Vespucci helped explore the eastern coast of South America and reached the mouth of the Amazon River. His travels also took him throughout the Caribbean, including trips to Cuba, Hispaniola, and the Bahamas. In 1501 Vespucci sailed along the South American coast to within 400 miles (640 kilometers) of its southern tip. In 1503 he took one more voyage and reached the Falkland Islands, off the coast of modern-day Argentina.

When he returned to Spain the following year, Vespucci not only spoke often about his travels, but wrote about them as well. One of his readers was a German mapmaker, named Martin Waldseemuller. In his writings, Vespucci claimed that he had captained ships to the

New World and bragged so much about what he had done there that Waldseemuller mistakenly thought the Florentine navigator had discovered the Western Hemisphere. In 1507, when Waldseemuller printed a wood block map, he placed the name "America" on modern-day South America.

A few years later, as Vespucci lay dying, he confessed he had not made the 1497 voyage and had only served as a ship's captain on one occasion.

Waldseemuller, realizing he had been mistaken about Vespucci's role in discovering the Western Hemisphere, tried to change the name he had given these new lands, but it was already well established.

In 1538 a Flemish mapmaker, Gerardus Mercator, produced a world map that included the two continents that Amerigo had boasted about discovering. On Mercator's map they are clearly labeled North and South America.

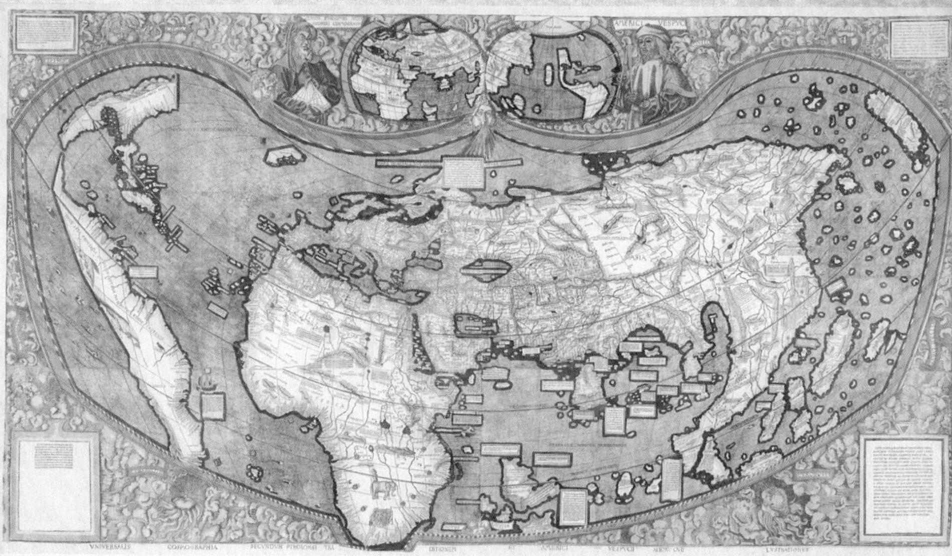

Map of the World, 1507. The map is accompanied by text explaining the use of the term "America" to describe the continent of that name, and a Latin translation of the four journeys of Amerigo Vespucci. A small portrait of Vespucci appears at the top of the map.

(continued from page 93)
pushing the ships along at a reasonable clip, and causing some of the men to wonder how they would ever get home safely to Spain and their families.

After three weeks, no land had been spotted, and some of the crew were becoming restless. As the weeks went by, with no land in sight, life aboard Columbus's ships became difficult. The food was monotonous, the drinking water tasted sour, and the ships were so small that most crew members had to sleep on deck.

"Land Ahoy!"

On October 9 some members of Columbus's crew began to threaten mutiny. The following day the winds blew mightily westward, driving the ships as never before. Fortunately for Columbus, at 2 A.M. on October 12 the lookout aboard the *Pinta,* Ridrigo de Triana, sighted what he thought was white cliffs in the distance. The captain of the *Pinta,* Martin Alonso Pinzon, also saw something and fired a cannon, the sign to the other vessels that land had been spotted.

Gray clay cliffs lay ahead, situated on a small Bahamian island, perhaps today's Watling Island. By noon on October 12, the last day to find land before they would have had to turn back for Spain, Columbus and his men dropped anchor and went ashore on the first land they had seen since leaving the Canary Islands, nearly five weeks earlier.

In the wet sand they dropped to their knees, many crying for joy, as Columbus named the island San Salvador, the Holy Saviour. But Columbus had not reached the Orient as he had planned. He had reached America.

Columbus and his men spent the following four months exploring the Caribbean, landing at other islands, including Hispaniola (today's Haiti and the Dominican Republic) and Cuba. As he explored, Columbus was curious why nothing resembled how he had imagined Asia, and why he found no rich kingdoms, flush with gold.

Later Voyages

Over the next 12 years, Christopher Columbus made three more voyages to the Americas (in 1493, 1498, and 1502), each time exploring a little more territory, and eventually reaching as far south as Brazil. He told the king and queen of Spain that the lands he had discovered boasted much gold and other metals, but he only delivered to their court exotic animals, a few gold trinkets, and some Taino natives he and his men kidnapped. In time, Columbus became frustrated with the lack of profits his voyages produced, as did the Spanish rulers.

In 1494 Columbus suggested the natives be made slaves for Spain, but Queen Isabella harshly rebuked him for the proposal. Eventually, however, the island natives were enslaved, forced to work and pan their own rivers for gold. Columbus died in 1506, frustrated, nearly penniless, but still convinced that he had reached the Orient, its riches hidden over just one more horizon.

9 Explorers and Conquerors

With Columbus's discovery of a vast, unknown land, the Spanish monarchy committed significant resources to exploration and colonization of this new territory. Between 1492 and 1504, Columbus completed four voyages to the New World. Others would follow in his footsteps, each making his contribution in extending Spanish power and in filling in the map of lands that had been previously not only unknown, but uncharted.

BALBOA AND THE SOUTH SEA

One such explorer was Vasco Nunez de Balboa. This Spanish soldier explored the mainland and is credited as being the first European to cross the continent, at the Isthmus of Panama (its narrowest point, in today's Central America) and reach the western waters of the Pacific Ocean.

Little is known of Balboa's early life, including the year of his birth, which may have been 1475. When the Spanish began sending colonists to the New World, Balboa became intrigued. He joined a Spanish expedition bound for South America in 1501. When his group of colonizers failed and returned to Hispaniola the following year, Balboa fell into heavy debt and worked as a pig farmer. In 1509 he tried to join another colonizing effort headed for South America, but his creditors would not let him leave Hispaniola.

Governor of Darien

The following year, a desperate Balboa hid as a stowaway in a flour barrel on a supply ship bound for Panama. When the ship reached the Panamanian port of San Sebastian they found the colony abandoned. Balboa, having explored to the south, suggested a colony be established there among Indians he knew to be friendly. Soon, they built the community of Darien on the west side of the Isthmus, with Balboa as its governor.

From the Indians, Balboa heard stories of a great ocean to the west. Curious, he led 90 Spaniards and several Indians across the Panamanian Isthmus, a difficult crossing, amid tropical heat and jungles filled with snakes and insects. After weeks of exploring, Balboa and his men were led to a mountain where they could gaze out to the west and view the Pacific Ocean. The former pig farmer and stowaway had made one of the most important discoveries for Spain.

Balboa's Fall

Difficulties continued to stalk Balboa, however. In 1514 he was replaced by another governor. When Balboa remained in the region of Darien, the settlement he had helped establish, the new governor took a disliking to him and falsely accused him of treason. Balboa was arrested and, following a show trial, he was found guilty. He was beheaded, and his head was put on a pike and displayed to the public.

With Balboa's discovery of the Pacific—waters he called the "South Sea"—it became clearer that Columbus had not reached the Orient at all, but had discovered a previously unknown landmass. However, this realization came too late to matter to Columbus. He had died seven years earlier.

FERDINAND MAGELLAN

Sometimes those who helped extend Spain's power in the Western Hemisphere were, like Columbus, not even Spanish. One such explorer was Ferdinand Magellan, the son of a Portuguese nobleman. In 1519 he led a convoy of ships that became the first sailing vessels in history to completely circumnavigate, or sail fully around, the earth.

Magellan believed he could reach the Moluccas, the Spice Islands of Asia, by sailing west across the Pacific. In 1519, sponsored by King Charles of Spain, he set sail across the Atlantic with five ships—the largest measuring 70 feet (21 meters) in length—and a crew of 240 men. Magellan sailed his fleet southwest to the southern end of South America and through the treacherous waters his men called *Tierra del Fuego* ("Land of Fire"). Here ocean currents and winds are severe. The crossing was so arduous that one ship, the *Santiago,* was lost in a storm and the crew of a second, the *San Antonio,* mutinied and turned back. Magellan was left with three ships, nervous crewmen, and the unknown waters of the Pacific, the largest ocean in the world, ahead of him.

As the weeks passed, Magellan began to realize just how large the Pacific Ocean really is. The trio of ships sailed for 98 straight days without seeing any land, except for a few uninhabited islands. Supplies ran perilously low. Finally, Magellan and his men reached the Mariana Islands in the South Pacific. Nearly all of them were starving and sick. After reaching the Philippines, which proved to the Portuguese sea captain that he had sailed completely across the Pacific and reached the Spice Islands, Magellan was killed on April 27, 1521 by local natives wielding spears and cutlasses.

Magellan's men were determined to continue their voyage back to Spain. They picked up a cargo of cloves and other spices in the East Indies, continued across the Indian Ocean to the southern tip of Africa, and arrived back in Spain on September 6, 1522. Of the 240 men who had set out with

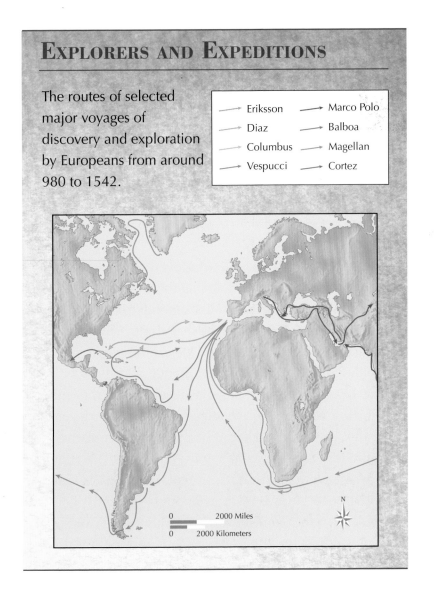

Explorers and Expeditions

The routes of selected major voyages of discovery and exploration by Europeans from around 980 to 1542.

Magellan three years earlier, only 18 remained alive! But these men had accomplished a great sailing feat, having completed the first successful circumnavigation of the earth.

EXPLOITING THE NEW WORLD'S PEOPLES

When Christopher Columbus made landfall in the Americas in 1492 he realized that the next step would be colonization. When he sailed back to Spain in 1493, he left crew members behind to man a settlement. But when Columbus returned later that same year with 1,000 excited colonizers, priests, and soldiers, they found the colony wiped out, its European inhabitants killed. Natives had turned on them because of poor treatment.

What would soon follow was a military conquest of the lands that Columbus had claimed on behalf of the Spanish crown. This included enslavement of the native peoples and exploitation of the natural resources found locally. A pattern of abuse and conquest on the part of the Spanish in the New World developed quickly.

First, the Spanish would "discover" a territory, with a population of natives already living there. The natives would often treat the new visitors well, thinking they might be gods or other powerful figures. In the meantime, Spanish soldiers would size up the Indians and determine what resources they would need to subdue them if necessary.

The Spanish would help themselves to the Indians' resources, including their food and women, then the natives, resentful and feeling taken advantage of, would carry out some random act of violence against the Spanish. In response, the Spanish would unleash their superior weapons—including guns, their ships, armor, even dogs—and crush all who resisted. Then the Spanish would take control of every aspect of their victims' lives, enslaving them and forcing them to work in their own silver and gold mines, with much of the

Exchange of Two Worlds

European contact with the Indian populations in the New World sometimes delivered a silent killer to those native groups in the form of germ warfare. The Spanish spread diseases that were common in Europe and might not usually kill their victims. But the Indians had no natural immunity because they had not been exposed to those germs before, so some illnesses, such as smallpox, spread rampantly, causing much death and destruction.

There was, however, another exchange between the Spanish colonizers and the American Indians, and one that was much more advantageous to both groups—food. When colonists made contact with the Indians of the Caribbean or on the mainland in Central or South America, they found the natives eating foods that were unfamiliar to them. The colonists tried these foods for themselves and liked what they ate. They then took them back to Europe, where some of these new plants—especially a variety of fruits and vegetables—became quite popular.

The exchange went both ways. Colonists were introduced to such new foods as potatoes, squash, pumpkins, corn (known to the Indians as maize), and tomatoes. Although Asian cotton had been traded with the Europeans for centuries, American cotton proved superior. In return residents of the New World saw their first lemons, oranges, coffee, sugar cane, wheat, rice, and lettuce.

There were also exchanges of animals. The horse had only existed in early, prehistoric America, and even then as a much smaller animal, more the size of a large dog. Europeans introduced horses to the Americas, as well as cows, chickens, sheep, and pigs. These animals provided the Indians with new sources of meat, hides, eggs, milk, and wool, and changed native cultures forever.

American tobacco became widely used in Europe, as well as other parts of the world. And two great New World tastes—vanilla and chocolate—also made their way to Europe through vanilla beans and cacao.

metal being sent back to Europe to enrich Spain and the Spanish monarch.

Land Grants

At the heart of this new economy in the New World, the Spanish established the *encomienda* system, which provided stability and regulation of Spain's new American colonies.

The *encomienda* was a land grant handed out to a Spanish colonial leader, which generally included a certain number of slaves to work his lands. The only obligation the proprietor had was to convince his native workers and slaves to convert to Catholicism. Not only did this harsh system oppress innocent American Indians, it also conflicted with the spirit of Christianity.

One person who tried to speak out against these abuses was a Spanish priest, named Bartolome de las Casas. In the earliest days of colonization on the island of Cuba, he had been passive about the destructiveness of Spanish colonizing. But, in later years, he spoke out against colonial policy, lamenting and criticizing Spanish leaders.

In writing about the abusive system, Father Las Casas noted in his *Short Account of the Destruction of the Indies,* that, while converting the natives to Christianity was still his primary purpose for being in the New World, "the means to effect this end are not to rob, to scandalize, to capture or destroy them, or to lay waste to their lands." The sympathetic padre also chronicled the destruction of the natives, estimating that the campaigns and wars fought against the original inhabitants of the New World had caused significant decreases in their populations.

Between 1519—the year the Spanish reached the mainland and marched on the Aztec empire—and 1605, the estimated native population of Mexico was reduced from 25 million to just one million people. However, the extreme death rates among natives following European contact was not the result, generally, of warfare. Instead, it was caused by the introduction of European diseases, such as smallpox, measles, and typhoid, to native groups who had no natural immunities to these deadly germs and viruses. Also, even before the Europeans arrived, native empires such as the Aztecs were in a weakened state as a result of prolonged environmental issues, social disruptions, and political rivalries.

CORTES AND THE AZTEC

As the Spanish established their New World colonies, they were led by several key motivators. Many of them believed that their first goal was to convert the native peoples to Christianity, but a significant number were also interested in the potential riches of the New World. Stories circulated of a great kingdom to the west, in modern-day Mexico, where a powerful, wealthy people named the Aztec lived in an extensive civilization, perhaps the most advanced in the Americas. The Spaniard who first made contact with them was one of the second wave of adventurers to arrive in the New World—Hernando Cortés.

Born in 1485 in the Spanish town of Medillin, Cortés left for the New World at 19 years of age, landing on Hispaniola in the West Indies in 1504. As a successful soldier, he gained an *encomienda* and at the age of 34 was chosen to lead a military expedition into modern-day Mexico, in search of the fabled Aztec empire. After spending time on the mainland, Cortés realized that the Aztecs believed him to be the god Quetzalcoatl (ket-sahl-koh-ahtl) who, according to the Aztec calendar, had appeared decades earlier and was scheduled to return as part of a 52-year cycle. When the Aztec emperor's representatives arrived with a great disc hammered out of gold and a helmet filled with gold dust, Cortés knew he was marching toward a kingdom of great wealth.

On August 8, 1519, Cortés and his men were outside the Aztec capital of Tenochtitlán, where Mexico City stands today. As the city came into sight, the Europeans gazed in wonder at what lay before them. Tenochtitlán was a "floating city," covering five square miles (13 square kilometers), situated in the midst of a vast lake, its buildings and temples forming a massive checkerboard, set off by stone streets and canals filled with boats. There were floating gardens on the lake, and great pyramids of white stone gleaming in the sun. This New World wonder was home to perhaps 300,000 Aztec, including the Emperor Moctezuma, who had no choice but to recognize Cortés as the rightful ruler of his lands, and offer himself to the Spanish, who took him prisoner.

With the residents and leaders of the city convinced that the Spanish were powerful gods, they treated them well—at least, at first. The Spanish were appalled at the Aztec practice of human sacrifice and ordered the building of a Christian church, which the Indians helped to construct. Priests would educate the Aztecs in Catholic ways.

Then, a local tribal chief brought to Moctezuma the head of a Spanish soldier who had been killed in an earlier battle, proving that the Aztecs were not dealing with gods at all, but men. Helpless, the Aztecs watched as Cortés's men began stripping their city of its gold, taking the precious metal and idols out of palaces and temples.

Retaliation

With tensions flaring and panic mounting, the Spanish began an attack on the Aztecs, who responded in kind. On June 30, 1520—known as the *Noche Triste,* or "Sad Night"—Cortés and some of his men were able to make it out of the city, but half of his men were lost.

Cortés had not seen the last of Tenochtitlán. In December 1520 he lay siege to the Aztec capital, finally forcing the

Dating from the early sixteenth century, this illustration of Mexico City, or Tenochtitlán, is probably based upon a sketch from Cortés's sketchbook. Built on an island in the middle of Lake Texcoco, the city had a grid of roads and waterways.

residents to surrender on August 23, 1521. To make certain his enemies would not rise against him again, he ordered his men to begin dismantling the city. The world of the Aztecs died, as the Spanish left hardly a trace of their culture, their architecture, or their religion.

A new Spanish empire was established, the Kingdom of New Spain. On the ruins of the once powerful city of Tenochtitlán, a new Spanish capital was established, Mexico City, and the Spanish gained an immense amount of land, adding it to their already vast holdings in the New World.

Cortés received great rewards for his successful subjugation of the Aztecs. For several years he lived in great luxury both in Spain and Mexico, but honor and riches did not remain. Fearing he might take more power, the Spanish authorities removed him from his position. In his last years he lived in virtual seclusion, dying in Spain in 1547, a bitter and lonely man.

FRANCISCO PIZARRO AND THE INCA

For years, the Spanish had heard rumors of a similar civilization south of Central America, a golden land called "Biru." By the 1520s, immediately on the heels of Cortés's destruction of the Aztecs, Spanish officials sent explorers south in search of the fabled "Biru."

One such conquistador was Francisco Pizarro. In December 1531, he and a force of 200 men set sail from Panama and landed months later along the Peruvian coast. Soon he was marching inland into the empire of the Incas, nestled in the Andean mountains of modern-day Peru. After capturing and killing the Inca leader, Pizarro and his men easily invaded their capital, Cuzco, and destroyed it in 1533. Pizarro took control of the Inca Empire, but within a few years, in 1541, he was killed in a sword fight by a rival conquistador, Diego de Almagro.

The Maya: Precursors of the Aztecs

The Aztecs were the dominant advanced culture in Mesoamerica at the time of Columbus' discovery. However, they were not the first such culture to have emerged in Mesoamerica. An even earlier people—the Maya—built intricately carved stone temples and pyramids and created a writing system.

The Maya lived in modern-day Mexico, Belize, and Guatemala, centered largely on the Yucatan Peninsula. Other Mayan villages were located in western Honduras and El Salvador. They may have been influenced by an earlier civilization, the Olmec, who had also developed a number and writing system.

Mayan culture emerged around 300 C.E. For the next thousand years, the Maya were the dominant force in Central America. Between 300 and 900 C.E. the Maya established elaborate cities, such as Tikal, located in the Guatemalan rainforest. Tikal comprised 3,000 buildings in its heyday, including six temple pyramids. Tikal also boasted shrines, baths, ballcourts, bridges, paved roads, palaces, monasteries, water reservoirs, aqueducts, vaulted tombs, and astronomical observatories.

Archaeologists have uncovered many Mayan items from the jungles, including jade carvings and masks, stylized painted pottery, ceramic figures of humans and of their gods.

Not only did the Maya create a written language, they also devised mathematics, accurate calendars, and astronomical studies. Their writing was based on hieroglyphics, or picture writing, as well as glyphs that represented a word or a sound. Even today cultural experts and linguists are still trying to decipher them all.

JUAN PONCE DE LEON

Born in 1460 in Spain, Juan Ponce de Leon accompanied Columbus on his second expedition to the New World in 1493. He became one of the first Europeans to reach the island of Borinquen, which would one day be known as Puerto Rico. De Leon set off to find a legendary place called

"Bimini," where the waters of a spring were said to provide eternal youth. During his explorations he reached the American mainland, a region he called *La Florida,* which means "land of flowers." De Leon visited Florida twice, in 1513 and then eight years later. On his second visit, he established a colony, bringing along 200 men and 50 horses onboard two ships. At one point, de Leon met with local natives at the site where the city of St. Augustine, Florida, is today.

Colonizing Florida did not go well for Ponce de Leon. Hostile natives attacked his party along Florida's west coast, and de Leon was shot in the stomach with a poisonous arrow. The Spaniards abandoned Florida and sailed back to Cuba, where Ponce de Leon subsequently died.

HERNANDO DE SOTO

Hernando de Soto was born between 1496 and 1500. As Pizarro's second in command, he discovered the great road that led the Spaniards directly to Cuzco, the Inca capital. However, De Soto did not approve of Pizarro's treatment of the Incas. He left the expedition and returned to Spain in 1536, rich from Inca gold.

With permission from Charles V of Spain, de Soto set out for Florida in May 1539, in the path of Ponce de Leon. For the following three years De Soto and his immense expedition sought another Aztec empire, a kingdom flush with gold, but no such place could be found.

Inland Explorations

De Soto and his men wandered for 2,000 miles (3,500 kilometers), traveling through modern-day Florida, Georgia, the Carolinas, Tennessee, Alabama, Mississippi, and Arkansas. He marched far enough north to reach the southern tip of the Appalachians. He was also the first recorded European to see the wide waters of the mighty Mississippi. Along the way, his party encountered several Indian nations of the Southeastern United States, including the Natchez. De Soto and his officers ruthlessly destroyed tribes, enslaved them, and even hunted them down for sport. His men also unwittingly spread deadly diseases. At times, when his men could not seize all the crops of a given tribe of Indians, De Soto simply let loose his herd of pigs to destroy the remainder.

Some of the Indians fought hard to stop De Soto's advance through their lands, especially the Coosas of northern Georgia and the Chickasaws of Mississippi. As a result of these battles, De Soto lost a large number of his men. Despite such losses and tribal conflict, the gold-hungry Spanish conquistador was driven constantly by his dream of greater wealth. In May 1542 he was overcome with an illness and died, his body buried along the banks of the river he had discovered—the Mississippi. Ironically, he had utilized one fortune in search of another that never panned out.

THE FIGHT FOR COLONIES BEGINS

Early Spanish explorers such as Cortés, Pizarro, and De Soto laid the groundwork for the spread of the Spanish empire in the New World. Throughout the sixteenth century the Spanish would create a great colonial world, one built on the backs of Indian labor and the accumulation of great wealth in gold and silver. But their power in the Americas would not go unchallenged. Within 30 years of De Soto's death, other European kingdoms, led by the English and French, would attempt to counter-balance Spain's wealth and dominance in the Americas, first by raiding Spanish outposts and treasure ships, then by establishing rival colonies of their own. The remainder of the 1500s and the early 1600s would witness great rivalries in the New World as Old World powers each tried to establish their own spheres of influence in the newly discovered continents of North and South America.

Chronology

30,000–8000 B.C.E. Pleistocene Era
12,000–10,000 B.C.E. Humans enter Western Hemisphere
10,000 B.C.E. Clovis Points come into use in North America. Earliest residents of California arrive
9500 B.C.E. Earliest humans occupying the Great Basin
9000 B.C.E. Early humans reach the eastern United States
9000–8000 B.C.E. Folsom Points are in use

TIMELINE

30,000–8000 B.C.E.
Pleistocene Era

12,000–10,000 B.C.E.
Earliest accepted era for humans entering the Western Hemisphere

1000 B.C.E.
People in Mexico develop small village systems. After a 5,000 year gap, Northeast Indians in place, experiencing Early Maritime Culture

1000 B.C.E.–500 C.E.
Early Woodland stage for Northeast Indians

30,000 B.C.E. — **1000 B.C.E.** — **500 B.C.E.** — **1 B.C.E.**

9500 B.C.E.
Earliest humans occupying the Great Basin region

7000 B.C.E.
Introduction of systematic agriculture in the New World

7000–500 B.C.E.
Archaic Era

500 B.C.E.–1000 C.E.
Plains Woodland Culture

300 B.C.E.
Southwestern peoples practicing agriculture and living in pit houses

100 B.C.E.
Southwestern residents making early forms of pottery

Chronology

9000–5000 B.C.E. Earliest occupants of the Southwest region and Great Plains

8000 B.C.E. Neolithic Era begins

8000–6000 B.C.E. Extinction of the Pleistocene Animals in the Western Hemisphere

8000–4500 B.C.E. Plano Points are in use by early Americans

7000 B.C.E. Evidence indicates early humans reach southern tip of South America.
Southwest Indians develop Desert Culture.
San Dieguito Culture develops in California.
Introduction of systematic agriculture in the New World

7000–500 B.C.E. Archaic Era

500 — 750 — 1000 — 1250 — 1542

300–900 C.E. Mayan culture reaches its zenith

700–1100 Third Anasazi culture era: Developmental Pueblo Period. During this era the people at Chaco Canyon reach their zenith

900 New wave of Eastern Woodland Indians arrive on the Great Plains

986 Norseman Bjarni Herjolfsson is blown accidentally to Canada

1000 Norseman Leif Eriksson lands on the Canadian coast

1200–1500 Aztec culture reaches its zenith

1271 Marco Polo reaches China with his father and uncle

1400s Haudenosaunee (Iroquois) establish Iroquois Confederacy

1492 Christopher Columbus reaches the New World

1519 Cortés enters the lands of the Aztec

1539–42 Francisco de Coronado explores the American Southwest. Hernando de Soto explores the American Southeast and reaches the Mississippi River

6000 B.C.E. Northwest Indians experience Coastal Land Hunting Period

5000 B.C.E. California's dominant Indian culture is the Desert Culture

5000–2500 B.C.E. Residents of the Great Plains largely abandon the region due to drought

3000 B.C.E. Northeast Indians develop a crude but systematic form of agriculture

2500 B.C.E. Natives of the Southwest begin to cultivate maize. Indians return to the Great Plains

2000 B.C.E.–1 C.E. Indians in the Great Basin region create sedentary village life

2000 B.C.E.– 500 C.E. Middle Period Culture in California

1000 B.C.E.–500 C.E. Early Woodland Stage for Northeast Indians

1000 B.C.E. People in Mexico develop small village systems. After a 5,000 year gap, Northeast Indians in place, experiencing Early Maritime Culture

500 B.C.E.–1000 C.E. Plains Woodland Culture

300 B.C.E. Southwestern peoples practicing agriculture and living in pit houses

100 B.C.E. Southwestern residents making early pottery

100 B.C.E.–400 C.E. Anasazi Basket Maker Phase

100 B.C.E.–700 C.E. Northeast Indians Middle Woodland Stage

300 C.E. Earliest Mayan culture in place

300–900 C.E. Mayan culture reaches its zenith

400–700 C.E. Second Anasazi era: Modified Basket Maker

700–1500 Southeast Indian Mississippian Culture

700–1100 Third Anasazi culture era: Developmental Pueblo Period

900 New wave of Eastern Woodland Indians arrive on the Great Plains

900–1150 Indians at Cahokia construct Monk's Mound

986 Norseman Bjarni Herjolfsson reaches Canada
1000 Norseman Leif Eriksson lands on the Canadian coast
1100 Mogollon culture building adobe structures above ground
1100–1300 Fourth Anasazi culture era: Gat Pueblo Period. During this period, Chaco Canyon is abandoned
1200–1500 Aztec culture reaches its zenith
1271 Marco Polo reaches China with his father and uncle
1298 Polo's book, *Description of the World*, is completed
1300 Anasazi cliff dwellers abandon Mesa Verde
1300–1550 Final Anasazi era: Regressive Pueblo period
1400 Mogollon culture gives way to the Anasazi
1400s Haudenosaunee (Iroquois) establish Iroquois Confederacy
1477 First printed edition of Marco Polo's book appears
1488 Bartolomeu Dias sails to southern tip of Africa
1492 Christopher Columbus reaches the New World
1492–1504 Columbus completes four voyages to the New World
1498 Vasco da Gama sails around Africa and reaches India
1507 Amerigo Vespucci reaches South America. Martin Waldseemuller uses the name "America" on a map
1513 Vasco Nunez de Balboa reaches the Pacific Ocean. Juan Ponce de Leon lands in Florida
1519 Cortés enters the lands of the Aztec
1519–1605 Native population of Mexico is reduced from 25 million to 1 million, largely by disease
1520 Ferdinand Magellan circumnavigates the globe
1521 Cortés subdues the New World Empire of the Aztec
1532–33 Francisco Pizarro defeats the Inca Empire in Peru
1539 Hernando de Soto explores the American Southeast and reaches the Mississippi River
1539–42 Francisco de Coronado explores the American Southwest

Glossary

Amerind The language that served as the linguistic stock for nearly all early American Indians. Anthropologists recognize ancient Amerind-speakers as the first wave of emigrants to the New World.

Anasazi The descendants of the ancient Southwestern Mogollon. The Anasazi culture lasted until 1550 C.E.

Athapascans The ancient relatives of the Navajo and Apache.

atlatl A prehistoric spear-throwing device with which ancient hunters achieved greater accuracy and velocity.

Beringia The temporary land bridge that linked the Western Hemisphere and Asia during the most recent ice age.

Cathay The medieval European name for modern-day China.

Clovis Point A type of early bifacial projectile point that was fluted at the base to a length of one-third that of the point.

counting coup The practice among Great Plains Indians of striking an enemy during battle, rather than killing him, for the purpose of humiliating him and gaining great honor. Coup is the French word for "blow" or "strike."

drakken A type of shallow draught boat, used by the Vikings, or Norsemen. The name comes from the Norse word for "dragon."

encomienda A land grant handed out to a Spanish colonial leader, which generally included a certain number of slaves to work his lands.

Five Civilized Nations A confederacy of Southeast Indian nations that consisted of the Cherokee, Chickasaw, Choctaw, Seminole, and Creek.

Folsom Point A type of early projectile point noted for its delicacy, with fluting running nearly the entire point's length.

Hispaniola Old name for the Caribbean island that is now Haiti and the Dominican Republic.

Hohokam An ancient Southwestern culture, centered in south-central Arizona.

hunter-gatherers Term used by anthropologists to describe nomadic, prehistoric peoples. The name refers to their chief means of supplying themselves with food.

Inuit Name given to northern American Indians, sometimes referred to as Eskimos.

maize Indian name for corn.

mammoth Prehistoric elephant-like beasts with long tusks. They lasted until the end of the Pleistocene Era, around 11,000 years ago.

mastodon Prehistoric elephant-like creatures from the Pleistocene Age that stood 10 feet (3 meters) tall and became extinct around 6000 B.C.E.

Mimbres A group of Southwest Mogollon peoples who produced a unique style of "black on white" pottery.

Mogollon Ancient Southwestern culture, centered in the southern half of New Mexico and southeastern Arizona. The culture formed by 1100 B.C.E. and lasted until around 1400 B.C.E.

Moluccas The Spice Islands of Asia's East Indies.

Na-Dene Second wave of ancient emigrants to the New World, who spoke a language stock by the same name.

Neolithic A Stone Age period spanning thousands of years until around 5,000 to 7,000 years ago. From *neo* meaning "new" and *lithic* meaning "stone."

Pleistocene Age The most recent ice age, which may have taken place between 30,000 years ago and approximately 10,000 to 11,000 years ago.

Pueblo Name for several groups of sedentary Indians in the Southwest, from *pueblo,* the Spanish word for "village."

sagas Norse or Viking tales, relayed as oral traditions. These stories were told over and over for hundreds of years and rarely written down.

skreelings A name given to American Indians by the Viking leader Leif Ericsson, which is translated as "barbarians" or "weaklings."

Stinkards The commoner class among the mound-building Natchez peoples.

tepee A cone-shaped dwelling constructed by Great Plains Indians, consisting of a lodge pole frame, covered over with buffalo hides.

Three Sisters The trio of crops commonly raised by American Indian farmers: corn, beans, and squash.

travois A wooden frame used to drag goods over land used by Native Americans.

Vikings Scandinavians or Norsemen who lived between 800 and 1100. Their name comes from the early Nordic word *vik,* which means a "bay" or "inlet."

Vinland A colony established by the Vikings along the coast of modern-day Newfoundland, Canada during the late tenth century. The site was uncovered in 1961 by a Norwegian archaeologist and is known as L'Anse aux Meadows.

Western Hemisphere The lands that comprise the Americas: North and South America and the islands that are strung throughout the Caribbean Sea.

wickiup A grass hut constructed by some American Indians for shelter.

Bibliography

Adovasio, J. M. with Jake Page. *The First Americans: In Pursuit of Archaeology's Greatest Mystery*. New York: Random House, 2002.

Bergreen, Laurence. *Marco Polo: From Venice to Xanadu*. New York: Alfred A. Knopf, 2007.

Bonvillain, Nancy. *Native Nations: Cultures and Histories of Native North America*. Upper Saddle River, NJ: Prentice-Hall, 2001.

Boorstin, Daniel J. *The Discoverers: A History of Man's Search to Know His World and Himself*. London: Phoenix, 2001.

Bushnell, G. H. S. *The First Americans: The Pre-Columbian Civilizations*. New York: McGraw-Hill Book Company, 1968.

Chapman, Carl H. and Eleanor F. *Indians and Archaeology of Missouri*. Columbia: University of Missouri Press, 1983.

Cumming, W. P. *The Discovery of North America*. New York: American Heritage Press, 1972.

Daniels, George. *The Spanish West*. New York: Time-Life Books, 1976.

Diamond, Jared. *Guns, Germs, and Steel: The Fates of Human Societies*. New York: W. W. Norton & Company, 2005.

Editors of Time-Life Books. *What Life Was Like When Longships Sailed: Vikings, AD 800–1100*. Alexandria, VA: Time-Life Books, 1998.

Folsom, Franklin and Mary Elting Folsom. *America's Ancient Treasures*. Albuquerque: University of New Mexico Press, 1993.

Gibson, Arrell Morgan. *The American Indian: Prehistory to the Present*. Lexington, MA.: D.C. Heath and Company, 1980.

Haynes, Keen. *A History of Latin America*. Boston: Houghton Mifflin Company, 2000.

Hoffer, Peter Charles. *The Brave New World: A History of Early America*. Boston: Houghton Mifflin Company, 2000.

Horwitz, Tony. *A Voyage Long and Strange: Rediscovering the New World*. New York: Henry Holt and Company, 2008.

Josephy, Alvin M., Jr. *The Indian Heritage of America*. Boston: Houghton Mifflin Company, 1991.

———*500 Nations: An Illustrated History of North American Indians*. New York: Gramercy Books, 1994.

Kehoe, Alice Beck. *North American Indians: A Comprehensive Account*. Upper Saddle River, NJ: Pearson, 2006.

Lamb, Susan. *Mesa Verde National Park: Life, Earth, Sky*. Mariposa, CA: Sierra Press, 2001.

Las Casas, Bartolome. *A Short Account of the Destruction of the Indies*. New York: Penguin Group Inc., 1992.

Lemonick, Michael and Andrea Dorfman. "*Who Were the First Americans?*" TIME, March 13, 2006, pp. 44–52.

Lowenstein, Tom. *Mother Earth, Father Sky: Native American Myth*. Amsterdam: Time-Life Books BV, 1997.

Mann, Charles C. *1491: New Revelations of the Americas Before Columbus*. New York: Vintage Books, 2006.

McNeese, Tim. *Myths of Native America*. New York: Four Walls Eight Windows, 2003.

Page, Jake. *In the Hands of the Great Spirit: The 20,000 Year History of American Indians*. New York: Free Press, 2003.

Perrigo, Lynn. *The American Southwest: Its People and Cultures*. Albuquerque: University of New Mexico Press, 1971.

Pritzker, Barry M. A *Native American Encyclopedia: History, Culture, and Peoples*. New York: Oxford University Press, 2000.

Roop, Peter and Connie. *I, Columbus: My Journal, 1492–3*. New York: Walker and Company, 1990.

Strutin, Michal. *Chaco, A Cultural Legacy*. Tucson, AZ: Western National Parks Association, 1994.

Further Resources

Aller, Susan Bivin. *Christopher Columbus*. San Diego: Lerner Publishing Group, 2003.

Bandon, Alex and Patrick O'Brien. *Travels of Marco Polo*. Orlando: Raintree Publishers, 2000.

Brownstone, David M. *Historic Places of Early America*. New York: Simon & Schuster Children's Publishing, 1989.

Croy, Anita. *Ancient Pueblo: Archaeology Unlocks the Secrets of America's Past*. Washington, D.C.: National Geographic Society, 2007.

De Angelis, Gina. *Hernan Cortes and the Conquest of Mexico*. Broomall, PA: Chelsea House Publishers, 1999.

Feeney, Kathy. *Marco Polo: Explorer of China*. Berkeley Heights, NJ: Enslow Publishers, Inc., 2004.

Green, Jen. *Encyclopedia of Ancient Americas*. London: Anness Publishing, Ltd., 2000.

Hinds, Kathryn. *The Vikings*. Tarrytown, NY: Marshall Cavendish, Inc., 1998.

McNeese, Tim. *Christopher Columbus and the Discovery of the Americas*. New York: Chelsea House, 2006.

———*Marco Polo and the Realm of Kublai Khan*. New York: Chelsea House Publishers, 2007.

Nicholson, Robert. *Vikings*. Broomall, PA: Chelsea House Publishers, 1993.

O'Neill, Dan. *The Last Giant of Beringia: The Mystery of the Bering Land Bridge*. New York: Basic Books, 2005.

Roop, Peter. *Christopher Columbus*. New York: Hyperion Books for Children, 2001.

Thomas, David. *Exploring Native North America*. New York: Oxford University Press, 2000.

Yolen, Jane and David Shannon. *Encounter*. San Diego: Harcourt Brace & Company, 1996.

Web sites

Library of Congress—Christopher Columbus:
http://www.loc.gov/exhibits/1492/columbus.html

Manitou Cliff Dwellings—Anasazi:
http://www.cliffdwellingsmuseum.com/anasazi.htm

Marco Polo's Asia:
http://www.tk421.net/essays/polo.html

National Parks Service—Bering Land Bridge National Preserve:
http://www.nps.gov/archive/bela/html/vvcenter.htm

National Parks Service—What is Beringia?:
http://www.nps.gov/akso/beringia/whatisberingia2.htm

Public Broadcasting Service—Conquistadors:
http://www.pbs.org/conquistadors/

Public Broadcasting Service—The Vikings:
http://www.pbs.org/wgbh/nova/vikings/

Silk Road Foundation: Marco Polo and His Travels:
http://www.silk-road.com/artl/marcopolo.shtml

The Bering Land Bridge Theory:
http://www.eckstein.seattleschools.org/elmiller/ss/land_bridge/

Picture Credits

Page

8: Istock © Steven Allan
17: NHPA/Daniel Heuclin
23: © Warren Morgan/CORBIS Inc.
35: Illustration by John James
38: Istock © Jeremy Edwards
43: Werner Forman Archive/ Peabody Museum, Harvard University, Cambridge, Ma.
55: Illustration by Mark Bergin
57: Stapleton/HIP/TopFoto
58: Werner Forman Archive/Field Museum of Natural History, Chicago
66: Werner Forman Archive/Field Museum of Natural History, Chicago
71: Werner Forman Archive/ University of British Columbia, Vancouver, Canada
78: © 2005 The Image Works/ TopFoto
83: World History Archive/ TopFoto
91: © 2003 Credit: Topham Picturepoint
95: © The British Library/HIP
107: World History Archive/ TopFoto
128: Courtesy of Abbott Studio, www.abbottsudio.com

Index

About the Author

Tim Mc Neeese is associate professor of history at York College in York, Nebraska. Professor McNeese holds degrees from York College, Harding University, and Missouri State University. He has published more than 100 books and educational materials. His writing has earned him a citation in the library reference work, *Contemporary Authors* and multiple citations in *Best Books for Young Teen Readers*. In 2006, Tim appeared on the History Channel program, *Risk Takers, History Makers: John Wesley Powell and the Grand Canyon*. He was been a faculty member at the Tony Hillerman Writers Conference in Albuquerque. His wife, Beverly, is assistant professor of English at York College. They have two married children, Noah and Summer, and three grandchildren—Ethan, Adrianna, and Finn William. Tim and Bev have sponsored college study trips on the Lewis and Clark Trail and to the American Southwest. You may contact Professor McNeese at tdmcneese@york.edu.

About the Consultant

Richard Jensen is Research Professor at Montana State University, Billings. He has published 11 books on a wide range of topics in American political, social, military, and economic history, as well as computer methods. After taking a Ph.D. at Yale in 1966, he taught at numerous universities, including Washington, Michigan, Harvard, Illinois-Chicago, West Point, and Moscow State University in Russia.